# Child Protection and Domestic Violence

*Thangam Debbonaire & Audrey Mullender*

LEARNING RESOURCES
CENTRE

Havering College
of Further and Higher education

VENTURE PRESS

Published by
VENTURE PRESS
16 Kent Street
Birmingham
B5 6RD

British Library Cataloguing-in-Publication Data
A catalogue record for this book is available from the British Library

ISBN  1 86178 042 7   (paperback)

Design, layout and production by
Hucksters Advertising & Publishing Consultants,
Riseden, Tidebrook,
Wadhurst, East Sussex TN5 6PA

Cover design by
Western Arts, 194 Goswell Road
London, EC1V 7DT

Printed and bound in Great Britain
by Biddles Ltd, www.biddles.co.uk

# Contents

*Children and domestic violence*                    **1**

*Children's experiences in their own words*         **15**

*Danger and safety (child protection)*              **19**

*Family support and working with women*             **31**

*Direct work with children*                         **49**

*Prevention and effective co-ordination*            **61**

*Bibliography*                                       **75**

# Children and domestic violence

## A CHANGING CLIMATE

**Over the past decade, concern has been rising about the welfare of children whose mothers are being abused. Research findings in Canada and the USA that indirect abuse (that is, the impact of living with abuse) can be as harmful as direct abuse (Jaffe *et al*, 1990), were followed by a growing recognition in this country that child care practitioners were not well equipped to handle such situations (Mullender and Morley, 1994; Farmer and Owen, 1995). This was mainly because domestic violence had not previously been on their professional agendas and most practitioners lacked the necessary knowledge and skills to intervene in appropriate and helpful ways. To make matters worse, social services departments were inclined to make the stock response that domestic violence was not their statutory responsibility and to discourage their staff from becoming involved with abused women.**

Now, all this has begun to change. The Department of Health (1998) has made the link between domestic violence and the needs of children and has funded the production of a comprehensive training pack (Hester *et al*, 1998 and 1999). Research in the UK context has demonstrated that professionals can learn to look out for domestic violence in child abuse cases and to respond more helpfully when they find it (Hester and Pearson, 1998), once they are given agency encouragement to do so. The practitioners with the longest experience of working with children who have lived with domestic violence, child workers in women's refuges, are beginning to be recognised as an important national resource (Hague et al., 1996). And children are beginning to be asked what they themselves would find helpful (McGee, forthcoming; Mullender *et al*, forthcoming).

## A COMPREHENSIVE RESPONSE

Though the issue of children and domestic violence is currently placed largely within a child protection context (Department of Health, 1998), it can usefully be considered more broadly. In keeping with current thinking about family support (Department of Health, 1995), this book will aim to explore, not only what happens to women and children, but also the best ways of meeting children's needs within a wider family and community context. It will make suggestions about the kinds of response that could make life safer for women and children. It will adopt a practical and readable approach aimed at the busy practitioner.

The most helpful response for children needs to relate to their whole situation and is likely to involve a combination of responding:

- more rigorously to the behaviour of abusive men;
- more sympathetically to abused women;
- both more actively and more reflectively to children who live in situations where their mothers are being abused.

Above all, this book will stress that

*'woman protection is frequently the most effective form of child protection'*,
**(Kelly, 1994, p.53, original emphasis)**

## A CHILD-CENTRED APPROACH: CHILDREN AS SOCIAL ACTORS

Even children who live in the most adverse circumstances cannot accurately be thought of as 'passive victims' or 'silent witnesses'. Children try to make sense of what is happening in their lives and do all sorts of things in the hope of making things better, including sometimes trying to intervene in the attacks upon their mothers or to summon help.

Sociologists nowadays recognise this and refer to children as 'social actors' or as 'having agency' in a situation – meaning that they shape the circumstances of their own lives as well as being shaped by them (James *et al*, 1998, p.6). Research, like practice, has progressed from being **about** children to being conducted **with** children.

Drawing on this and other work this book will be in tune with current calls for social work practice to be grounded in knowledge and evidence rather than in good intentions, outmoded theories or sometimes ill-founded professional assumptions. This is particularly important in the field of domestic violence which has been bedevilled by mythology for so long.

> *'She must have asked for it.'*
>
> *'I blame it on the drink.'*
>
> *'There's nothing social workers can do.'*

have been common responses. (See Mullender, 1996, for a rethinking of these dangerous inaccuracies.)

## WHAT IS DOMESTIC VIOLENCE?

> *Domestic violence is the use of physical, sexual, emotional and other forms of behaviour that hurt, frighten, injure or are forced, by one person (usually, but not always, a man) over another (usually, but not always, a woman) with whom the perpetrator has or has had a marital, sexual or other intimate relationship, by power in order to gain or maintain control.*

### POWER AND CONTROL

A useful way for practitioners to understand domestic violence – since it tells us what pattern to look out for – is as the misuse of power and the exercise of control by one partner over the other. The diagram of a 'power and control wheel' is becoming increasingly familiar to practitioners in this country. The detailed content of the diagram has been extended by projects in the UK and elsewhere in the course of their work, and a Canadian reworking of the original American version is shown overleaf.

**POWER AND CONTROL WHEEL**

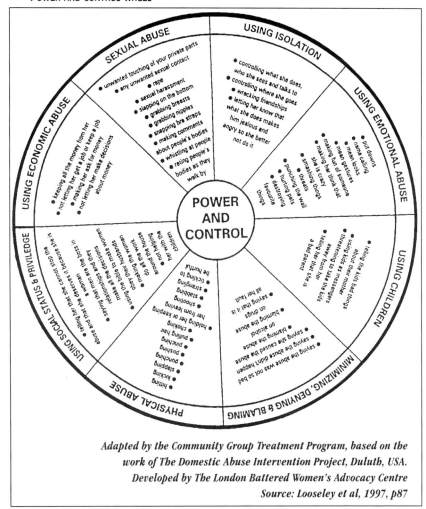

*Adapted by the Community Group Treatment Program, based on the*
*work of The Domestic Abuse Intervention Project, Duluth, USA.*
*Developed by The London Battered Women's Advocacy Centre*
*Source: Looseley et al, 1997, p87*

## A PROBLEM OF MEN?

The abusive pattern of power and control is usually
exercised by a man over a woman. It is not difficult to
understand its roots when we recall that men's control of
their wives' behaviour was not just socially condoned but
was an absolute expectation by church and state for many
centuries. Men were also given total domain over their
wives' bodies – the English courts have only accepted the
concept of marital rape since 1992. Before that, the law

assumed that women, on marrying, had no further right to refuse the sexual demands of their husbands.

These assumptions never worked the other way round. Even in cultures where mothers are at their most influential in the family, there is simply no history of women controlling the bodies and the lives of men purely on account of their gender, but there has been a very strong tradition in most religions and cultures of giving such rights to men over women (as long as they do not step outside other norms relating to ethnicity, socio-economic status and so on).

Though these attitudes have begun to change profoundly in more recent times, there are a number of reasons why domestic violence persists:

- some men appear to be unaware that times have changed;
- some men are deliberately trying to behave as if times have not changed;
- many women have been encouraged to believe that their partners are entitled to control or abuse them in all kinds of ways;
- help for women is still under-resourced and not everyone knows how to access it;
- society's attitudes towards the changing status of women are profoundly ambivalent so that 'men behaving badly' are often the butt of humour rather than revulsion, and there are persistent attempts (overt or covert) to 'keep women in their place';
- the authorities, including the courts, which could do the most to impose sanctions on abusive men are often the most male-dominated and the most resistant to thoroughgoing change;
- the relevant legal and policy changes are comparatively recent and practice will take time to catch up.

Despite directives from the top, change may be slow to come at the operational level and may also be jeopardised by gaps in the system. For example, there is a complex chain of events that has to happen from the police being called, arrest of the man, laying of charges, prosecution, conviction, to effective sentencing. Much can, and too often does, go wrong along the way.

For all these reasons, even if there is a situation where a

practitioner comes across a man claiming to be hit by a woman, he or she should ask:

- is this a man making exaggerated or false claims to conceal his own abusive behaviour?
- is this a woman hitting back when undergoing abusive attacks?
- or is this truly a situation in which the woman is exercising ongoing domination over a male partner through violent means.

And, even were the latter to be the case, it would not carry the same social messages or be subject to the same social toleration as a man abusing a woman. Indeed, women tend to be treated more punitively. So it is our clear view that there is not an 'equal and opposite' woman-on-man version of domestic violence and we will only be using the term to describe a hitherto socially condoned pattern of men controlling women by the threat or use of violence.

Abuse also occurs in same-sex relationships. Homophobia and heterosexism can make it unsafe for lesbians and gay men to seek help or action against the abuser as the abused person may be revictimised by those who are meant to help them. Similarly, black women may face or fear racism and unhelpful assumptions about them and their partners when they seek help. Consequently, though abuse is always wrong and always harmful, and practitioners should never silently tolerate it, our responses to it need very careful thought where it does not follow the statistically normal pattern of male abuse of a woman or where there is an interplay with other forms of oppression. The persons experiencing the abuse usually know best what is likely to make the situation safer or more dangerous.

## HOW COMMON IS DOMESTIC VIOLENCE?

- As many as 1 in 3 women (with similar rates across all social and ethnic groupings) admit having experienced some form of domestic violence other than being grabbed, pushed or shaken (Mooney, 1994; see also summary of statistics in Hester *et al*, 1999).
- About 2 women a week are killed by men with whom they are (or have been) in an intimate relationship (Home Office, Criminal Statistics for England Wales, 1992ff).

- This accounts for almost half the women who are killed in this country, with strangulation being the most common cause of death. In contrast, less than 10 per cent of men killed are killed by female partners or ex-partners, often in self-defence after long-standing domestic abuse by the man.
- These figures only represent those incidents for which the man is successfully prosecuted and may, therefore, be an underestimate.
- Abusive men use many ways to frighten women (such as driving recklessly, pushing them downstairs) which could mean that there are deaths in road-traffic accidents, accidents in the home, as well as suicides, which are actually the result of domestic violence.

Contrary to the impression given by the media, it is far rarer for a woman to kill a man than *vice versa*. Also, since women kill their abusers when in fear of their own lives, both groups of deaths in fact result from men's violence to women, not from an equalising of violence between the sexes. Yet, because of the way the law works, women who kill their abusers have been more likely to be convicted of murder and to serve much heavier sentences because 'provocation' and the use of weapons have been thought about in terms of what happens between men having a fight, not in relation to women in long-standing fear defending their lives (Radford, 1992.)

The messages for practitioners are:

- When a woman says her abuser has threatened to kill her, she must be believed.
- There is no way of knowing in advance which man could kill or which woman may die.
- The only safe way to proceed is to work on the basis that any intervention undertaken with any family where there is a woman being abused may be on a 'life and death' basis (usually with the woman likely to die, but occasionally the man).
- Consequently, levels of confidentiality and support must take into account this degree of potential danger and its dreadful repercussions for the children.
- Even if your agency really cannot help (and this is less often the case than is claimed), an abused woman should never be sent away not knowing where to turn.

## WHY DOESN'T SHE LEAVE?

To many people who have not lived with domestic violence, it seems obvious that a woman could, and even should, leave as soon as she is first attacked. This is a gross over-simplification of women's lives and is also ironic, given how recently women were still being advised to 'stay for the sake of the children' (Maynard, 1985).

Amongst the many reasons why women stay with or return to violent men (NCH Action for Children, 1994) are:

- They believe the violence is a 'one-off' or, later, that the man can change.
- Later still, when they know the full extent of the danger, women may be terrorised into staying by their abuser threatening to kill them if they go.
- Men are, in fact, at their most dangerous when women try to end the relationship (Wilson and Daly, 1992) and some women have said that they prefer to have the danger close at hand and in a familiar form than to be looking at every shadow, never knowing when the man may next appear.
- It is common for the abuser to threaten to harm the children if the woman ever tries to leave him.
- Leaving involves giving up home, belongings, every aspect of daily life. For women who have worked hard to create a nice home for their family, it means sacrificing everything.
- Many women, especially those with very young children or with several children, have nowhere to go and cannot see how they could afford to live.
- Even now, many women do not know about refuges so it can be very important for practitioners in all settings to be able to advise them how to get help.
- Women resist uprooting their children and disrupting their schooling. For children with special needs, there may be complex arrangements in place which have taken much battling to obtain and which might be impossible to replicate elsewhere. Nevertheless, it is often when women realise their children are being adversely affected, or when they learn about direct abuse of their children, that they do decide to leave (Hester *et al*, 1994).
- Even then, leaving is often a process rather than an event. It may take several attempts before the woman is sure that things at home will not improve and that she can find a way to survive as a lone parent. It may then take some time to obtain ➤

> ◄ housing and the other provision she needs for herself and her children.
> - Current negative social attitudes towards single parents and emphasis on 'the family' make it harder for her to be sure she is doing the right thing.
> - Her own relatives, faith or community may be putting great pressure on her to hold her marriage together.
> - After family and friends, a woman typically contacts many other agencies for help but often without finding the assistance she needs (Dobash *et al*, 1985. Mullender, 1996).
> - She is also leaving a man she has loved or still loves and, frequently, it is the violence that women want to see ended, not necessarily the relationship.

Eventually, however, an abusive man kills his partner's love for him and may well kill her too unless she can get to safety. And, throughout all this, it must be asked why we expect the woman to leave, rather than the man to be controlled or removed. After all, when women leave them, abusive men are simply free to continue their abuse in new relationships.

## HOW DOES DOMESTIC VIOLENCE AFFECT CHILDREN?

There are well established links between domestic violence and concerns for the welfare of children. These encompass risks both of direct and of indirect harm.

### RISKS OF DIRECT HARM

Research in the UK has found that at least a third of children on the Child Protection Register have mothers who are being abused (London Borough of Hackney, 1993). This degree of overlap between the abuse of women and that of children doubles when experts look for it (Farmer and Owen, 1995) or when they help child protection professionals to re-examine their cases (Hester and Pearson, 1998).

This means that as many as 2 out of 3 child abuse cases could have domestic violence also present. The presence of one should always be a good enough reason to look for the other and for ensuring that the safety of both the woman and the children is actively considered. In cases where children have died (O'Hara, 1994) or where child protection practice has failed to make children safe (Farmer and Owen, 1995), violence towards the children's mothers has not only been particularly likely to be present but has too often been dangerously overlooked in assessing risk and planning intervention. In fact, domestic violence often coincides with children being at the greatest risk of physical harm. There is also evidence to suggest a raised incidence of child sexual abuse (Forman, 1995; Hester and Pearson, 1998).

Other ways in which children may be at direct risk of harm include:

- threats from the abusive man to hurt or kill the children in order to coerce the woman to meet his demands.
- the abuser forcing the children to participate in abusing their mother.
- abused women themselves punishing their children more harshly than normal to forestall a worse beating from an abusive man, or
- abused women lashing out when 'at the end of their tether'.
- risks to unborn children. Violence may commence or escalate during pregnancy (Mezey, 1997), with injuries to the abdomen being a common occurrence. Stanko *et al* (1998, p.24) mention 2 per cent of women in a doctor's waiting-room survey reporting a miscarriage as a result of violence.
- children at risk of accidental injury, either because they get in the way of an attack upon their mother or because they frequently try to protect or help her.

### RISKS OF INDIRECT HARM

- Most children know their mother is being abused (NCH Action for Children, 1994).
- They see or hear much of what takes place because they are present or nearby (Hughes, 1992).
- They are often much more aware of the abuse than their parents realise (NCH Action for Children, 1994).
- Some children have seen their mother killed.
- Children may be profoundly affected by living with domestic violence. One Canadian study showed 2.5 times the rate of  ➤

- ◀ behavioural and psychological problems of other children (Wolfe *et al*, 1986).
- ● Children's lives may be disrupted by being forced to leave home, sometimes repeatedly, with the consequent impact on schooling, friendships and contact with wider family networks.
- ● There may be additional issues for black and other ethnic minority children who move away from a local community which may have offered some protection against racism (Imam, 1994), who encounter discriminatory attitudes when they and their mothers seek help (Mama, 1996), or who may be at risk of abduction from overseas.
- ● Children's needs may be neglected while their mother is in no fit state, physically or emotionally, to attend to them or while her abuser prevents her from doing so, though this is likely to improve once the woman is safe (Wolfe *et al*, 1986).

## THE IMPACT ON CHILDREN

There is no one syndrome. Each child reacts in his or her own way according to age, stage and circumstances – the youngest often through their health or development, older ones in emotional and psychological responses because they understand more of what is happening. Social workers are already skilled in looking for distress and disturbance in children, whatever form these may take, and should be well equipped to detect children being affected by situations of domestic violence. The difference will lie in learning to ask about what is happening to the child's mother, as well as to the children themselves, and in thinking about the safety of both as closely connected.

One should not make a blanket assumption that all children are badly or permanently affected. Children, even in the same family, can respond very differently, despite living in the midst of the same or very similar events. Some children have enough personal resilience or protective factors in their lives to cope. Children can also recover once they feel safe (Wolfe *et al*, 1986).

In one family of three sons, the eldest tried to fight his father as soon as he was big enough to do so and the youngest would run to seek help for his mother, while the middle one retreated into depression – making a full recovery only years later when his bullying and violent father was no longer in his life. The differences between the boys derived from their individual personalities and coping strategies, as well as their ages. They also give the lie to earlier assumptions about gender-specific reactions. In fact, the middle boy felt that he should have been able to 'act the man' but it was not in his make-up to do so. (See Morley and Mullender, 1994, for a detailed exploration of research findings which show no evidence that children respond in fixed ways or that they automatically grow up to repeat a pattern of abusive relationships.)

## HOW SHOULD WE RESPOND?

Domestic violence is everybody's business. The days of choosing not to intervene between husband and wife, or of dismissing an abusive attack as 'just a domestic' are over. Domestic violence has profound consequences in the lives of individuals, families and communities. It can lead to the deaths of women and children and to physical and emotional scars which may leave permanent damage. Mental health can also suffer.

The revised version of *Working Together* (Department of Health, 1998) recognises the relevance of domestic violence in child protection policy and practice. It emphasises the need for effective inter-agency co-operation across these two fields of work, including between domestic violence forums and Area Child Protection Committees. Beyond this, domestic violence should be included in every children's services plan as a grounds for considering the children who live with it as being 'in need' under the Children Act 1989. At the individual team and practitioner level, it should be something that is routinely asked about (with due attention to confidentiality and safety), about which statistics are collected, and which is seen as an integral part of child protection and child care practice. It should not, however, lead to a blanket child protection response.

Later chapters of this book will consider how children can have access to family support services and direct work to meet their own needs, as well as how they and their mothers can be effectively protected.

In such a complex area of intervention, there are no easy answers and no two cases will be alike. Nevertheless, to try and highlight the dilemmas in practice and the safest ways of becoming involved, we will follow a case example through every chapter. This will enable us to illustrate some of the key points raised at each stage of the book. Here we introduce the family, the domestic violence that is beginning to occur, and the impact it is having on the different family members.

---

**Case Study – Part 1**

Teresa Bennett (30) is married to Steve Bennett (26), a factory worker. Teresa has two children by previous relationships and is expecting twins in three months time.

Sally Smith, aged 14, attends Sacred Heart School where she enjoys sports and art. She wants to work in fashion.

Tommy Smith will soon be 5 and has just started attending St Joseph's School.

Teresa and Steve got married two months ago, when they knew Teresa was pregnant. They have known each other for several years, initially as part of a crowd of friends, and have lived together for fifteen months. Teresa's wedding to Steve was the big romantic day she had always dreamed of. From the first day he moved in with her, Steve has constantly brought Teresa little presents and he always takes her out on a Friday night. Teresa's mother, Molly Smith, lives nearby and is always willing to babysit.

Late one Friday evening, a few weeks after their return from honeymoon, Teresa and Steve have a blazing row and he punches her, causing her to fall backwards and bang her head. He accuses her of smiling at a man in the pub and calls her a 'slag'. Nothing she can say will make him believe that her behaviour has been just as normal and that she loves him.

Next day, Steve is enormously sorry and comes back from watching football with a bunch of red roses. He promises he will never do it again and sits cuddling Teresa on the settee all evening. Although she still feels dizzy and is rather worried about her unborn babies, Teresa agrees to make love when they go to bed because she is afraid of what Steve will do if she refuses. Steve is a bit less considerate than usual but goes to sleep in a good mood and also wakes up happy. He brings Teresa tea in bed and she decides that the whole thing has been a 'one off' and resolves to put the incident behind her. She will do her best to be a good wife and mother and she is sure that she can keep Steve happy in future.

On the Monday, Teresa's midwife tells her she is doing absolutely fine and does not appear to notice the bruises on Teresa's face. Nor does she give Teresa any openings to talk about the things that are worrying her. Teresa's mother dismisses the whole incident as 'just part of married life' and tells her she will have to learn to live with it.

Although Sally was upstairs in bed at the time, she heard her stepfather shouting at her mother on Friday night and her mother crying. She also saw her mother looking ill and worried next day so she was immensely relieved when they 'made up' at Saturday teatime. At school on Monday, her best friend, Carla, says she is sure there is nothing really wrong because Steve is so nice to everyone. Even so, Sally can't sleep for a few nights, lying awake listening for raised voices, and she does her best to be extra helpful at home so that she won't be the cause of any rows. She also tells her boyfriend, Mick, that he had better make sure he never shouts at her if he wants to keep on going out with her. She is fine at school, though, and gets top marks in a class project.

Sally decides her brother Tommy is too young to talk to about what has happened. He stayed to sleep over at his grandmother's on Friday, remaining there most of Saturday to play with his cousins. All he wanted to know when he got back was what was for tea and whether his favourite programme was on TV. In the days that follow, he is completely preoccupied with his new school friends and with pestering his parents to give him a puppy for his birthday.

Teresa is relieved that the children seem unaffected by what has happened. She does everything she can to hide her own worries from them (she is sure they don't know what happened) and to preserve a peaceful atmosphere in the family. Although Steve has accepted the children and loves them, Teresa realises he is very young to take on the responsibility of bringing them up. He gets fed up with Sally's boyfriend troubles and the hours she spends on the phone to her friends, while Tommy tends to be at his most difficult just when Steve comes home from work, tired and hungry. Teresa loves her kids to bits and wants them both to have more chances in life than she ever had. She also wants her marriage to work and the family's life together to be happy, like the families she sees on TV.

## Questions about the Case Study

1. *Is this domestic violence?*
2. *Who is the source of risk and to whom?*
3. *Is Teresa right to think that the children are unaffected by what Steve is doing to her?*
4. *What more, if anything, could the midwife have done?*
5. *Could anything be done about Steve's behaviour?*

# Children's experiences in their own words

*I lived with domestic violence. Sometimes it was frightening, sometimes I felt very scared and angry. Other times we did normal, family things, like having birthday parties and going out for the day and it was good. So my life wasn't all fear and fighting, and I'd say that that's probably true for a lot of the other kids here in the refuge. I don't want to go back and I'm not ready to see him yet but I expect that I will eventually – he's my dad, whatever he's done. My mum's just brilliant, she understands how I feel though my sister doesn't.*

**(boy, mixed parentage, aged 15)**

*It was very scary, my dad shouted and threw things and my mum cried a lot and tried to hide it from us. We went back to him soon after we left because my sister missed dad and neither of us could go to school where we were. And because mum was still very sad and wanted dad to be nice again. Then we went back and for a while it was OK but not for long and then one day mum collected me and my sister from school and said we were leaving for good. I was pleased because mum had been hurt by him, I think, and I was scared of him but my sister cried. Now mum is worrying about what will happen when dad wants to see us.*

**(girl, Asian, aged 8)**

*My first memory is of waking up when I was 4 and seeing my dad standing over my mum and punching her repeatedly in the stomach. We moved city eventually to get away from him. My mum wasn't a perfect mum and all three of us ended up in care, but I respect her for*

*trying to make things work and since we've all grown up
a bit we get on a lot better with her. But him, I have no
respect for – not only did he terrorise her, he didn't care
what happened to us, which she did.*

**(young man, aged 19, white)**

*I hate him for hurting my mummy and upsetting
everybody and wish he would just leave us alone. But
also he is my brothers' dad and I don't want to leave [city
child lives in] so I don't know what will happen. Last
time he tried to upset mummy it was on her birthday and
I shouted at him to go away.*

**(girl, white, aged 7)**

*I remember waking up to hear noises and words that I
didn't understand at the time but I knew that it meant
my dad was doing something to my mum that made her
very frightened. Later on I worked out he was raping her
or something like it – what she said stayed with me and
made sense when I got older. I remember hearing a loud
crash in the middle of the night once and then next
morning seeing a hole in the sitting room window and a
mark on a heavy glass paperweight which had been
moved.*

*Later my mum made a joke about him throwing it at
her and being a lousy shot. He could have killed her and
that must have been what he wanted to do. He was
always in charge of everything and used to do as he
pleased, but my mum, she never seemed cowed down by
him, but he very clearly controlled so much of her life. He
was also a lovely man very often. It must have been a
great struggle.*

*My mum and I have never talked about this aspect of
their marriage although we're very close and we've talked
about just about everything else. From the way she talks
about herself I don't think she would describe herself as
having been abused; what concerned her most, then and
now, was that by separating from my dad she deprived us
of a father.*

**(woman in twenties, mixed parentage)**

*I miss my daddy. I can't ring him because I don't know where he is. Maybe he will come and find me.*

**(girl, aged 7, white)**

---

**Case Study – Part 2**

Three weeks later, Steve hits Teresa again, while they are having a row about Sally staying out late the night before. This time he kicks her in the abdomen while she is on the floor and slams out of the house. Sally and Tommy are in their bedrooms and are very frightened. When she picks herself up, Teresa grabs a few things and takes the children to her mother's. There isn't really room for them and her mother tells her she has only herself to blame for letting Sally go a bit wild when she did not have a father's influence. She tells Teresa to go back to her husband.

Teresa would like to ask the midwife whether her babies are OK because of where Steve kicked her, but she is scared the other children will be taken into care if anyone in authority finds out. She is beside herself with worry but she has an antenatal appointment due soon and decides to hang on until then. They are bound to tell her if anything has gone wrong. If the bruises are still showing by then, she will tell them she tripped over Tommy's bike and fell heavily on the handlebar.

After a couple of days, during which Steve has rung constantly and sent flowers with a little note covered in kisses, Teresa goes home. Steve promises faithfully that he will never lay a finger on her again. He is true to his word but he expects everything to run like clockwork in the house, forces himself on Teresa once or twice when she really does not feel like having sex, and glares at her when she tries to express an opinion. He also starts passing remarks about how she can't even bring up her own kids properly and she must be stupid.

Over the next few weeks, Tommy starts having nightmares and wets the bed twice. Steve is furious when he finds out and slaps Tommy's legs. Sally stays round at her friend's house as much as she can, saying they are doing their homework together because Carla has a computer.

Teresa begins to feel overwhelmed and very confused as to what to do for the best. She is worried about her babies, worried about Tommy and Sally, and now quite frightened of Steve. But she also wonders whether everyone is right and it's her fault for not turning out to be a very good wife.

**Questions about the Case Study**

*1. What* would *happen if someone 'in authority' found out about this situation?*

*2. How helpful would this response be for Teresa? For the children?*

*3. What are the dangers and the options for Teresa and the children right now?*

# Danger and safety (child protection)

**This chapter shows how children living with or leaving domestic violence are at potential risk of harm to their safety and/or welfare. It explains how these risks may be directly caused by the domestic violence or by the process of leaving it. It also highlights how the child protection and civil court procedures that are intended to protect children often fail to do so for children living with domestic violence.**

Where one parent is being abused by the other, any process of child protection can in many cases undermine rather than support the safety of the non-abusing parent and consequently risk affecting the safety and welfare of the child. This can be due to agencies or individuals failing to identify the risks to the non-abusing parent, interviewing parents together so that the woman does not feel safe to speak, holding case conferences with both parents present so that again, the woman's participation is limited or contradicts what she may have said before. Because those agencies and individuals also fail to recognise the continued and often increased risk of violence after separation from the abuser, this is an added risk to the welfare of the children who have to move away because of domestic violence. If child protection work fails to identify the existence of the risks presented by leaving as well as living with domestic violence, this often results in failure to protect the children and it is therefore vital to identify who is doing what to whom and to ensure that the non-abusing parent is as supported and safe as possible.

There are links between the abuse of women and the abuse of children (see Kelly, 1994, for review of available research and practice implications; see Humphreys, 2000, for a review of actual practice in a local authority). It is clear then that wherever abuse of either a child or a woman is known about, the existence of the other should be explored, in ways that support and empower the non-abusing parent. The laws, policies and procedures for protecting children can and should still be used where necessary, but procedures for finding out if the mother is also being abused, and for working with her if she is, can and should be incorporated into these. A framework for doing this is presented in this chapter.

The needs and specific experiences of black and Asian women affected by domestic violence are often misunderstood or even overlooked (see Mama, 1996; Humphreys, 2000). Some staff may make inappropriate and unsafe assumptions about black people in general or about specific communities that may lead them to make decisions that provide black women with a lower level of protection and help than other women facing equivalent risks (see Mama, 1996 and Debbonaire, 1998). Outside agencies may believe that consultation with 'community leaders' is an appropriate process for developing responses to domestic violence in black and Asian communities. Too often, these so-called community leaders are unelected men with no mandate to represent women's experiences and needs. This then results in further assumptions being made about black and Asian women experiencing violence.

Children are sometimes used as interpreters when their mother's first language is not English. This is not appropriate for their welfare and may threaten their safety. It is also important to ensure that other interpreters are not a possible source of further risk to the woman. Ideally, all council interpreting services should be available on demand to meet the needs of a woman living in the area who is in need of help, and from an interpreter who has had training in domestic violence awareness. Some local authorities are now starting to adopt this approach.

It may be unsafe to use an interpreter who is part of the woman's own local community. They may be open to pressure from, or already connected to, individuals or views from within that community which may put her safety at further risk.

Immigration law means that some women have fewer

rights than others and are therefore at greater risk (Imam, 1994; Mama, 1996). Women who have entered the country only on the basis that they are married to someone with a right to remain in the UK cannot leave their husband within one year of arriving here without losing that right to remain. (Exceptions can now be made in cases of violence, but evidence is demanded which not all woman can produce and the process may take many months.) They and other women, such as refugees, may have 'no recourse to public funds' stamped in their passports, which means they cannot claim benefits or housing until their independent right to remain has been established. Some women may not have their own passports or may have been told by their abuser that they cannot ask anyone for help. These women are still entitled to police and court help but may not know how to go about getting it or be prevented from accessing it. It is therefore vital to get legal advice for any woman who is unsure of her immigration status.

Often, women and children are effectively left to contain the violence themselves (Farmer and Owen, 1995). Sometimes staff are afraid of the abuser and rightly so. It is consequently important to liaise with police about support and protection procedures and to ensure adequate staff supervision.

## SUMMARY OF RISKS TO CHILDREN FROM DOMESTIC VIOLENCE

This section presents the information given in the first chapter (*Children and domestic violence*) about children's experiences of domestic violence as summaries of possible risks to check for when assessing how far a child is at risk of harm in current and possible future situations. These can then also help to form a care plan which clearly sets out how each of these risks will be dealt with. They should also act as a reminder to deal with the potential risks to children and women when leaving domestic violence. These need to be heeded when working with a woman who is reluctant to leave and addressed if and when she does decide to leave.

All of the risks listed in this section do affect some children experiencing or leaving domestic violence and are attributable wholly or partly to these experiences.

However, they are only indicators to check for and should not be assumed to exist for all or even most children affected by domestic violence. Nor is the list comprehensive.

LIVING WITH DOMESTIC VIOLENCE: SUMMARY OF RISKS TO CHILD SAFETY
The risks often apply whether or not the man is living in the house.

- Sustaining injury or being threatened when trying to intervene;
- being hit by objects (perhaps aimed at their mother);
- having to leave the house to get help or stay out of the way;
- being injured pre-birth or as a babe in arms when the abuser attacks the woman;
- being abused directly, usually by the abuser, but possibly by the victim or other family member;
- being forced to take part in the abuse (including sexual) of their mother.

LIVING WITH DOMESTIC VIOLENCE: SUMMARY OF RISKS TO CHILD WELFARE AND DEVELOPMENT

- Restricted access to food, health care and clothes if the abuser controls money and movements;
- being unwilling or unable to bring friends home;
- having to appear in court as a witness;
- erratic attendance at school (if mother can't take child, if child fakes illness to stay at home and so on);
- living with tension and conflict, which they may only partially understand;
- being given a distorted perspective on relationships, rights and responsibilities;
- confusion/distress/torn loyalties.

LEAVING DOMESTIC VIOLENCE: RISKS TO CHILD SAFETY

- Continued threat to child and parent from abuser: he may know where they are if he is granted a child contact order, if they stay in the family home, or if he pressurises ➤

- family and friends to tell him. He may use other means to trace them;
- increased risk to children's health and safety of living in temporary accommodation – children living in bed-and-breakfast have significantly higher rates of accidental injury, compared with other children. They may be sharing accommodation with others who are risks to their safety. Facilities for washing, cooking, eating may be unhygienic or dangerous;
- if the child has disabilities and home and surrounding environment have been adapted to suit his/her needs, it may be difficult or slow to replace this in temporary or permanent accommodation. Statements of Special Needs are sometimes used by abusers to trace children and so also their mothers;
- risk of being traced via the child's school – even if the child changes school, the abuser may get information via child contact proceedings. School then becomes a site of risk, of violence, harassment and abduction for the woman and children.

## LEAVING DOMESTIC VIOLENCE: RISKS TO CHILD WELFARE/DEVELOPMENT

- Residence in bed-and-breakfast accommodation usually means lack of privacy for children with nowhere to do homework or see friends and a difficult journey to school;
- the woman's financial circumstances may change in ways that affect children, for example, reduced income may mean fewer/no school trips, no extra-curricular activities; conversely the woman gaining control over her own income may mean having these for the first time;
- disruption to a child's education – it takes time in some areas to get a new school place, the new school may work to different exam syllabuses, the school may be difficult or expensive to get to from bed and breakfast/refuge;
- the child may be the subject of child protection investigation which can be distressing, confusing and stressful.

The child's teacher, refuge children's worker, health visitor, nursery or playgroup leader and other family members have an ongoing relationship with the child and may be able to give information or provide specific support or help that cannot be gained elsewhere. Leaving violence is a positive development for children (provided it does not present new risks) but they or their parents may need practical help and emotional support to deal with experiences and particular needs.

### SECONDARY AND LONGER TERM EFFECTS OF DOMESTIC VIOLENCE

As discussed in the first chapter (*Children and domestic violence*), no fixed assumptions should be made about the long-term impact of domestic violence. Some children may display stress-related symptoms such as anxiety, tension, depression, sleeplessness, poor concentration, headaches, bed-wetting. Some children can experience a form of post traumatic stress disorder. These conditions will need to be identified and addressed to promote the child's safety and welfare. Other children with similar experiences of domestic violence may not display these symptoms.

Children and young people may develop behaviour patterns as part of making sense of or dealing with their experiences. Some of these behaviours can be potentially damaging to the children concerned. They may include eating disorders, self-harm, drug or alcohol abuse, truancy and running away from home. Again, many children who have lived with domestic violence will not develop these behaviours.

Few childhoods anywhere are without distress of some form. Children can, and do, develop ways of making sense of and coping with very difficult and upsetting experiences. These strategies can be built on and supported. Many children experience domestic violence and say that their lives are not dominated by the experience. There is a variety of reasons for this: parents may go to great lengths to ensure this, the violence may be sporadic; the children may be old enough to have independent social lives and the presence of other significant adult family members or friends may be a protective factor.

Appropriate and timely support and intervention is very likely to have a positive impact on the child's life and his/her relationship with the non-abusing parent (and possibly with the abusing parent). Children gain their understanding of relationships, rights and responsibilities at home not just from their parents but also from a variety of other sources.

Support and protection for non-abusing parents, particularly where they themselves are at risk of abuse, should be seen as an integral aspect of protecting a child. However, inappropriate or badly timed support and intervention can exacerbate risks and undermine the child, the mother, or the relationship between the two.

## DOMESTIC VIOLENCE IN CHILD PROTECTION WORK

Research with NSPCC child protection staff shows how a greater understanding and awareness of domestic violence can lead to an improvement in child protection overall, as well as noticing again the links between domestic violence and child abuse (Hester and Pearson, 1998).

This section outlines how this can work in practice. It presents two flow charts for use in child protection work to take account of the risks of domestic violence.

The first explains how to respond to the needs of women and children when domestic violence is known about.

The second explains how to deal with the possibility that domestic violence is taking place in families where it is known that a child is at risk of abuse.

The information following these two flow charts gives suggestions on how to assess the various risks involved and how to plan responses to these.

| Know about domestic violence? | In all cases, if possible | Ensure woman has adequate access to appropriate information and support |
| --- | --- | --- |
| Investigate if there is a child at immediate risk of significant harm | IF YES → | Use child protection procedures and make support and safety for the non-abusing parent an essential feature of this by:<br>● Working with non-abusing parents separately, offering information, support, access to other services, time to talk etc.<br>● Considering appropriate challenges to abuser<br>● Considering separate meetings including case conferences, so that abuser and non-abusing parent meet with staff separately |
| IF NO | | After risk of significant harm is reduced or removed |
| Investigate if there is a child in need as defined under section 17 of the Children Act | IF YES → | ● Work with the non-abusing parent, giving support, advice, referral to other agencies as appropriate, give basic legal information etc<br>● Monitor change, especially any increase in risk to child and non-abusing parent |
| IF NO | IF NO ← | Is child in danger? |
| ● Offer referral and appropriate information as safely as possible to the non-abusing parent<br>● Keep records of what is done by your agency<br>● Monitor if possible | | IF YES ↓ |
| | | Use child protection procedures and make support and safety for the non-abusing parent an essential feature of this |

**Figure 3.1**

| Know about abuse of a child? | In all cases ⟶ | Investigate risk and intervene in line with child protection procedures |
|---|---|---|
| ↓ | | |
| Always investigate if woman is experiencing domestic violence | IF YES ⟶ | Continue with child protection procedures and make support and safety for the non-abusing parent an essential feature of this by:<br>● Working with non-abusing parent separately, offering information, support, access to other services, time to talk etc.<br>● Considering appropriate challenges to abuser<br>● Considering separate meetings including case conferences, so that abuser and non-abusing parent meet with staff separately. |
| IF NO ↓ | | ↑ |
| Continue child protection processes, remembering that domestic violence may still be there. | | ↑ |
| ↓ | | ↑ |
| Remain alert to possible signs of domestic violence and continue to ask as, when and if appropriate. | IF YES ⟶ | ⟶ ↑ |

**Figure 3.2**

Finding out if there is domestic violence, identifying the perpetrator of domestic violence and attempting to work separately with the victim(s) can present problems for both the social worker and the abused woman concerned; it depends on the extent to which the abuser exerts control and the level of risk he presents. Caution is advisable to maintain safety for staff and service users. This means being aware of the risks domestic violence presents and taking practical steps to remove or reduce them.

### FINDING OUT IF THERE IS A NON-ABUSING PARENT WHO IS EXPERIENCING DOMESTIC VIOLENCE:

- Ask her – remember that many women will not call their experiences 'domestic violence';
- ask the children, again remembering to avoid jargon and to use clear terms;
- ask other relevant agencies, for example police or health visitors;
- remember you are not seeking proof beyond reasonable doubt;
- use your knowledge of impact of domestic violence on adult and child survivors;
- look for signs of one partner controlling the other;
- look for the existence of some of the consequences of living with domestic violence such as those listed below, for example by contacting school or health visitor.

### CONTACTING NON-ABUSING PARENTS SAFELY:

- Ensure that you contact ther woman separately if possible, stating that this is standard procedure in case her partner is suspicious;
- use another professional who is already in contact with the woman, such as a health visitor, who will not attract suspicion from the abuser;
- when phoning, ask if her partner is in the room and if she is free to talk;
- suggest an alias she can use for you if necessary;
- do not use letters unless agreed beforehand and there is reason to believe she and she alone will open them.

### ASSESSING THE POSSIBLE CONSEQUENCES OF DOMESTIC VIOLENCE FOR CHILDREN

Look for evidence of any of the risks listed above. Methods for doing this, in addition to the usual child protection investigation procedures, could include those listed for finding out whether domestic violence is present.

### BEING CLEAR ABOUT WHO IS THE SOURCE OF RISK

Throughout child protection processes where there is domestic violence, professionals should move away from the attitude that *'there is someone here who is failing to protect the children'* (which usually places responsibility for the violence on the victim) and towards 'there is someone here who is choosing to use violence, sometimes in the presence of the children' (which places responsibility on the abuser).

## LEGAL INTERVENTIONS

The full range of child protection and other related procedures can be used, including applications to court for assessment, supervision and care orders (section 47 and subsequent sections, Children Act 1989). Following the addition of sections 38A and 44A to the Children Act 1989 by schedule 6 of the Family Law Act 1996, it is now possible to exclude an abuser from the family home, if he is a risk to the child, whilst an interim care order or emergency protection order is in force, thus allowing the child and mother to remain in the family home. Social workers can also give women information about, and support them through, the process of using other legal options listed in the following chapter. In some cases, witness protection programmes organised by the police may be needed, particularly where the abuser is being prosecuted but is not in custody, or where he has relatives who may be a risk to the woman or children. The civil law relating to contact and residence (section 8, Children Act 1989) may often cut across all of these interventions. The legislation itself may be at fault (see Humphreys and Mullender, forthcoming) but the problem may also lie in its application, or often the lack of communication between professionals involved in the different aspects of law relating to children in these situations. As recent research suggests (Humphreys, 2000), women are still being warned that their children will be removed if they remain with or return to their partners; however, this practice is virtually pointless if the courts themselves then require the woman to deliver her children to contact meetings with the source of risk that the social workers are warning her to stay away from. Child protection interventions should wherever possible avoid making the woman responsible for the violence that her partner is using and instead adopt more focused approaches.

## CONCLUSION

Domestic violence presents risks for the women experiencing it, the children living with it and the professionals involved in dealing with it. There are clear and identifiable risks for children that social workers can look for when assessing children's lives. Existing legal provision and child protection procedures can be used and adapted to take account of domestic violence so that all child protection work is improved and more women and children are protected effectively. The next chapter presents ways of working with non-abusing parents to promote their own safety and welfare and that of their children.

---

### Case Study – Part 3

Teresa has reached the end of her tether. One night, after the pub, Steve came home and really laid into her, then raped her in the kitchen. She was too frightened to run away afterwards and, anyway, she had the children to think about. But, since then, her love for Steve seems to have shrivelled up and died and she knows now that something drastic will have to happen. She tries to think straight, but she has no money, no job, nowhere to go, and she daren't tell anyone what has been going on because Steve has threatened to kill her if she does. In any case, her family all think he is Mr Nice Guy and that it must be her fault if she can't keep him happy. The only way out she can see is to kill herself and hope her mother will bring up the children. Then she remembers the twins. So even suicide is not an option. She feels like an animal in a trap.

Then, one day, Sally comes home from school and finds her mum crying. She calls Steve a vicious b—d and he gives her a powerful slap round the face that sends her flying across the room. Sally runs out of the house screaming. That night, she does not come home but Steve will not let Teresa go and look for her, saying Sally is an unmanageable little 'slag' and deserves all she gets. Teresa is frantic with worry.

Finally, at about midnight, Carla's mum phones to say Sally has turned up there and she will bring her home in the morning. She can stay there for the night. Teresa can't sleep for worrying that Carla's family will find out what has been happening and report her to social services.

---

### Questions about the Case Study

*1. If, as a social worker, you did get to hear about Teresa's situation, what could you do?*

*2. Is Teresa right to feel scared about social services finding out?*

*3. What could social services do to change its image so that abused women would not be afraid to ask for help?*

# Family support and working with women

**The focus of this chapter is on practical and other ways to support and empower the non-abusing parent. The importance of doing this was established in the previous chapter where risks to be aware of were outlined. The process of a woman deciding to take action, including separating from an abusive partner, can take a long time and involves many different decisions. The woman may have to tell her story to many different people – to family, to staff in different agencies, in court, and so on; this in itself can sometimes be very distressing. Those trying to support the woman may be able to help by liaising with relevant staff in other agencies when necessary, providing this would not create further risks for her.** The principle of partnership between parents and social services that the Children Act (1989) formalised is clearly welcome and necessary. However, in cases of domestic violence it is vital to assess how to work in partnership with two parents who are not in an equal partnership themselves. This may mean ensuring the woman's safety and putting her interests before those of her abuser, undertaking separate work with both parents, changing how case conferences are handled, and building in support for the non-abusing parent as a central principle in child protection work. It is also important to be aware of the risks to the safety of the woman and her children that continue after separation from the violent partner (see previous chapter).

Research on crisis intervention with women experiencing domestic violence (Kelly, 1999) shows clearly that many women experiencing domestic violence make permanent decisions to separate from violent partners or take other steps to improve their safety if they are given information about their rights and what is available to them at the right time and without being judged. Research on interventions in police stations (Kelly, 1999) shows that this can often happen at a crisis point. If women experiencing domestic violence are given the right support and help at the right time, and especially when they ask for it, they can often make major changes in their lives that increase their own and their children's safety. Staff should be wary of making conjectures about whether a particular woman is likely to separate permanently from her partner at a particular time.

The provision, funding and support for Women's Aid refuge and other services, including outreach and aftercare and work with children, should be seen as vital for any range of services wishing to take domestic violence seriously. In addition to the provision of emergency accommodation, advice and support, Women's Aid provides an invaluable monitoring service for other agencies – they are able to pinpoint exactly where the processes involved (going to court, dealing with housing, applying for benefits, changing schools and so on) present risks for both women and children. The specialist work with children is also a central part of the services refuges provide.

Other independent advocacy services for women are also useful, especially if there is no refuge provision in the area or if there are particular needs to be met. For example, specific support groups, or specialist advice services for particular groups of women experiencing domestic violence, such as black women, women with disabilities, lesbian women, travelling women, refugees and so on, allow these women to get the advice and information that is appropriate to their needs and experiences, from specialist staff.

The woman may need support with safety planning. Even if she leaves her partner, he may be able to contact her: he may trace her or be given information which leads him to find her. She may, in any case, be fearful that he will trace her. It is important to take these fears seriously and possibly also to identify potential dangers that she may not be aware of. For example, court appearances are likely to be unfamiliar and the woman may need information about what will happen and about potential risks from her abuser. Child contact orders may reveal the woman's whereabouts and put her and possibly the children in further danger from her abuser (Hester and Radford, 1996). If you know that this is so, it may be appropriate for you to liaise with the Court Welfare Officer assessing the case and give them any information you may have about the risks to the woman and her children of inappropriately arranged contact.

## SAFETY PLANNING WITH WOMEN

Women who are still living with their abuser may need to work out a safety strategy for themselves and for their children (Kelly, 1999). This is a way of helping the woman to identify risks and ways of dealing with these and to plan for emergencies. Safety planning is also vital for women whose partners are attending a programme to change their violent behaviour. For some woman, it will make them realise that they are not safe in their current situations and need to change them. However, a woman who has left or evicted her abuser is often still at risk, sometimes of even more severe violence. It is therefore important to ensure that there are strategies for promoting her safety whether or not she lives with her abuser. Safety planning can help a woman to:

> - identify the places and situations where she may be (or feel) at risk from her partner;
> - increase her knowledge of the practical and legal safety strategies that may be appropriate for her;
> - identify ways of increasing her feelings of safety and well-being in her everyday life;
> - identify what help she can expect from your agency;
> - identify what she and others can do if her partner abuses/threatens her again.

## WAYS OF DOING THIS

Work at the woman's pace and from her own understanding of her experiences and the strategies she already has or starts to develop herself for dealing with the violence. Try to ask open questions about when and where and in what situations she feels safest and least safe. This will help both of you to identify what makes those places and times safe or unsafe and work out how, if at all, safety can be increased and risks reduced or removed.

Give her any information about practical ways of making her home or daily routine safer (see below). You may be able to advise her about where she can obtain financial assistance for this (for example the housing department or police Domestic Violence Unit). She will have her own ideas about what she needs. Use these as the starting point and make sure that she feels in control of the process. It is important not to make her feel that her life is being taken over by you as well as by her abuser.

Emphasise that what she is doing is all part of the process of making a safe new life for her and her children. Before she leaves, agree on times for future contact between you and her, arranging code words or other security measures for this if she is still living with her abuser. The risks of further violence to her, particularly if he discovers that she has involved others or taken steps he does not want her to take, mean that you must continue to ensure that she feels confident that your help is not going to make things worse. It could also put you at risk, so do some safety planning for yourself.

Be aware of the additional impact that racism has on black women and mothers of black children and of the effects that racism can have on the services and help they receive (Imam, 1994). You will need to be aware of assumptions that you may make about a black woman, and support her if she has to challenge those made by others. Some black women will be reluctant to seek the help of the police, for example, if they have fears of a racist response. Do not assume that you know better: try to work with the woman to find safety strategies that are appropriate to her, and remind her of her legal rights to protection from the statutory agencies she may be afraid of.

POSSIBLE CONTENT FOR SAFETY PLANNING SESSIONS WITH A SURVIVOR
OF DOMESTIC VIOLENCE

The following questions can form a structure for a session
with a woman on safety planning.

- Is she still living with her abuser?
- If not, does he know where she is living?
- Does she think that he will attempt to find her? Has she had threats from him in the past that he would?
- Are there ways she can think of that he might find out? (prompts: relatives of his or hers, friends, being followed from work or school, places he will know she has to go, address revealed on any official documents).
  Are there particular places she feels unsafe or safe? Can she say why? Can the unsafe aspects be minimised in any way? Is it possible for her to avoid these places? If it isn't possible to avoid them, how can she reduce the risks? Can she take someone with her, carry a mobile phone, let someone know where she is going, and so on?
- How safe does she feel today, right now?
  Ask her about the layout of where she lives. Where are the entrances and exits (including windows)? Where could he get in? Where could she get out? Where are the telephones? Is there a neighbour who she trusts to tell about the situation? Could this neighbour hear if she shouted? Call the police? Come round quickly if she felt frightened? If she still lives with her abuser, ask about parts of the house where she feels most at risk or particular times or situations that scare her (remembering not to give the impression that, if she tries to 'avoid trouble' by doing what he wants or fitting in with his demands, she will be safe).
- Are there places she still has to go (school, doctors, benefit offices and so on) that he might know about? Does she think that he might follow her there?
- Where and how will you next be in contact? Will this be by telephone or in person? What precautions do you need to take, if any, to ensure that this contact doesn't put her or you at risk?
- How does she feel now (as she is finishing the session)?

## PRACTICAL ISSUES TO COVER IN SAFETY PLANNING

The following information and guidance may assist the safety planning (please note that this list is not exhaustive):

### HOUSE

Things that the woman can do (perhaps with your help):

- check for window locks and for where she keeps the keys for these (important for fire emergencies as well as safety from abuser);
- check where children can get out and how easy this would be;
- agree on code words or other arrangement to use with the children if she wants them to get out, get help, or call the police;
- after evicting a partner, change the locks (some councils will do this for free in these circumstances);
- keep spare sets of keys at trusted friends' houses;
- consider keeping important documents and/or money at a trusted friend's house in case of emergencies.

Things that you can do:

- ensure that, on application forms for re-housing, the woman is clear about areas where she would not be safe and that she says why living there would present risks to her or her children;
- put her in touch with agencies such as Victim Support who can install alarms. There are different types available for different situations, for example, if she is still living with her partner or for after she has left.

### PHONES

Since the introduction of 1471 as a call return number and itemised phone bills, phones offer abusers more ways to keep track of who their partner is talking to or receiving calls from.

Things that the woman can do (perhaps with your help):

- dial a neutral number after any call to you or to similar agencies that she feels may put her at risk if he knows about it. This will only provide some temporary protection (as he cannot trace the call immediately) but if he has access to an itemised bill he may then be able to tell which numbers she has called. It is possible to stop itemised phone bills, but this may arouse the abuser's suspicion and is only possible if the woman is the account holder;
- put certain key numbers on the phone memory if this feels safe, so that she will be able to ring quickly.

Things that you can do:

- make sure that she knows that your number has a block on it so '1471' won't work;
- arrange code words so that when you telephone she can let you know when he is in the room or house, and if she is at risk and wants you to call the police;
- encourage her to make this arrangement with any friends or family she can trust who may phone her;
- ask her if it would also be useful for the older children to know of this arrangement.

## REGULAR ROUTINE

If she hasn't moved away or has stayed locally, her regular routine may present risks to her safety or that of the children. Things she can do (perhaps with your help):

- vary her route to work;
- ask her colleagues not to accept phone calls from her abuser;
- explain to people at her place of religious worship why they must not give her partner information about her whereabouts;
- talk to her family and friends about what they can do if he tries to find out from them where she is;
- think about whether there is anyone else associated with her abuser who may also be a risk to her and try to ensure they are not given information about whereabouts;
- talk to her children about what they can and cannot tell their father if they are in contact with him. You may be able to help with this (see below).

Things that you can do:

- ask if he has ever threatened to hurt her or the children if she should try to leave. Remember that many men do carry out these threats, particularly if they realise that their partners are not going to return to them;
- advise her on legal steps that she can take if she fears that her partner will abduct the children; and put her in touch with a solicitor.

### EMERGENCY CONTACT NUMBERS

Check that she knows who to call at night, how she can get police and refuge help, how to contact you again, how to give information to any men's programme he may be attending if he becomes violent or threatening.

### BASIC LEGAL RIGHTS AND SERVICE PROVISION

**NOTE:**
**This is a guide for basic information only. Please consult a solicitor or other relevant person in actual cases.**

### WOMEN'S AID SERVICES

Refuges are safe places where women and children can go if they are experiencing violence from a known abuser, for a break, for respite, for the first stage of a permanent move or for whatever they need. They can get advice, support and specialist services for children as well as accommodation and help with moving on. Women's Aid national helplines deal with referrals to refuges across the UK. There are separate offices in England, Scotland, Wales and Northern Ireland and also several regional referral offices, including Manchester and Nottingham. (Referrals in London are dealt with by Refuge, which is a separate organisation.) Refuges also give outreach help and advice to those who don't need accommodation, and aftercare to those who have moved out of the refuge. Women's Aid also provides a national information and training resource, campaigns and works for changes in law and practice, and promotes the issue of domestic violence publicly to raise awareness.

### PROTECTION UNDER THE CIVIL LAW

Women can apply to the court for occupation orders or protection orders (Family Law Act 1996) if they or their children are under threat of violence or harm. Protection orders tell an abuser not to do something (hit, hurt or threaten and so on). Occupancy orders specify who should and who should not live in the house. They will usually also order the abuser not to come near the house or enter it. Each order lasts for a specified period of time but can be renewed if there is still a need. Since 1997, powers of arrest are automatically attached to the order unless the victim(s) will be sufficiently protected without this. This means that the police can arrest the abuser for breach of the order alone, even if what he has done does not constitute an offence (eg going too near the house).

If the abuser has never lived with the woman, it is usually possible to use the 'stalking' legislation to provide civil protection (Protection from Harassment Act, 1997). In certain circumstances, it may be possible to oust the abuser (though only temporarily) from his own home if there is a child living there who is made the subject of an emergency protection order or interim care order (Family Law Act 1996, Schedule 6, introducing sections 38A and 44A to the Children Act 1989).

### POLICE HELP

Women can always dial 999 in an emergency and sometimes neighbours or children may do this. Depending on the circumstances, the police may be able to arrest and remove the abuser for breach of the peace, criminal damage, harassment or other offences such as actual or grievous bodily harm. They can usually help a victim to safety if that is what she wants. Most police forces now have domestic violence units (DVUs), or a similar unit that also handles child protection or other violent offences, staffed by specialist officers, to provide a dedicated co-ordinated response to domestic violence. They can give women information about whether they can press charges and what this means, assist with going to court, keep them informed of the process of a case, help them to contact refuges and other agencies, and so on. All police forces are required to have a policy on domestic violence and to specify how officers should respond to this type of crime.

### CRIMINAL PROCEEDINGS

The violence may constitute actual or grievous bodily harm, rape or other sexual offences. The offender will then usually be arrested and charged. The Crown Prosecution Service will decide whether there is sufficient evidence to prosecute. This does not necessarily have to depend on the woman agreeing to this, although she will usually be the main witness. Threats to kill and other threatening behaviour may also constitute an offence. A solicitor or the police DVU will advise. Evidence such as photographs of damage to person or property, medical records, statements from neighbours and family or police witnesses, as well as evidence from the women and children can all be useful. You should always record information about any attacks, threats or injuries you have witnessed.

### HOUSING

Women experiencing violence or the threat of violence and who have children or are pregnant are in priority need and are entitled to be re-housed by the local authority (Housing Act 1996). However, this can take some time and may be difficult to obtain. In the meantime they are usually entitled to temporary accommodation which can be a refuge. The woman may be entitled to housing benefit to help with this. Housing benefit can also sometimes be paid on two properties at once, if necessary, for a short period. Women who have financial interests in, or who are the sole owners of, the family home must register their interest in the property in order to stop it from being sold behind their backs. It is important to consult a solicitor. Women who are joint tenants of a council or housing association property may be able to apply to have the tenancy transferred to them alone. Women with no children may have to wait longer or may not be entitled to permanent accommodation. Women with no legal right to reside in the UK cannot be granted public housing until they have obtained leave to remain; some local authorities will process an application for housing in the interim and this saves time.

## MONEY

Women who have no other source of income can apply for benefits, including housing benefit. However, this can sometimes take time and women with no recourse to public funds (see p42) will not usually be able to claim. Married women can apply for maintenance, property or other financial settlements if they are separating permanently. Unmarried women are sometimes able to do this too. Women may get legal aid for advice about financial settlements, unless they are on Income Support, in which case this will usually be handled by the Child Support Agency (CSA).

## CHILD SUPPORT AGENCY (CSA)

Women who fear that harm or distress to themselves or their children may result from a claim being made by the CSA to an absent parent do not have to authorise the CSA to pursue this claim. If a woman refuses to authorise the claim in these circumstances she should not be penalised for this. There is a space on the CSA forms to declare this and to state the reasons. Any proof she has of the violence is always helpful but not usually essential.

## DIVORCE

Women who are married to their partners can apply for a divorce, usually using the fact of cruelty as grounds for stating that the marriage has irretrievably broken down.

## LEGAL AID

Women who have low incomes can apply for legal aid to pay for a solicitor. Anyone, including those who are not entitled to Legal Aid, can go to a solicitor who is part of the 'Green Form' scheme and get a free initial consultation. Usually, individuals will have to pay the first twenty-five pounds of legal costs.

## CONTACT WITH THE ABSENT PARENT

In most cases, if an absent parent applies to the court under section 8 of the Children Act 1989 for contact with his/her children he/she will get it. The court's guiding principle is the welfare of the children and they will appoint a court welfare officer (CWO) to investigate the child's circumstances and prepare a report. There is an assumption that contact is almost always in the best interests of the child and there is, therefore, a need to prove otherwise if this is not the case. The CWO will always interview both parents, children deemed old enough and sometimes other people concerned. Any parent has the right to be given a separate interview with the CWO. Home Office guidelines (Home Office, 1994) now require CWOs to be mindful of the effects of domestic violence and the safety needs of victims.

### WOMEN WITH UNCERTAIN IMMIGRATION STATUS

Women with no independent right of residence in the UK can only remain in the country as long as they are living with their husbands during their first year in the UK. This means that they may face deportation if they leave them during this time, even for reasons of violence.

However, many Women's Aid groups and other organisations will support these women and help to find money to support them and their children. For example, one group obtained money from the local authority fund (section 17, children in need) as defined in the Children Act 1989 to pay for food and clothing for a family, as the children were living in the local authority area and were therefore their legal responsibility.

### PROTECTION FROM CHILD ABDUCTION

There are civil and criminal measures that can be used to try and prevent children from being abducted or to recover and return children after they have been abducted. Any woman who fears that her partner will attempt to abduct her children, particularly if he has the means of taking them out of the country, should consult a solicitor about the various options. Other practical measures can also help. Women should take birth certificates, passports and other legal documents with them when they leave their partner, notify the school of the risk and ask them not to let younger children leave with anyone other than named persons, have a stop put on applications for copies of the child's birth certificate (a solicitor or law centre will advise on how to do this), and consider moving the family to a part of the country where there are no connections with the abuser.

The Children's Legal Centre and ReUnite, the organisation for parents of children who have been abducted, are also good sources of information and support.

## LEGAL ADVICE

Relevant legal advice is available from local law centres, the Rights of Women legal helpline, the Children's Legal Centre helpline, and specialist solicitors, particularly those recommended by local women's groups. Make sure that any solicitor consulted specialises in this complex area of law. Incorrect or inappropriate advice can be not just unhelpful but dangerous.

## GENERAL ADVICE

Remind women to take all legal and other important documents when they leave home, whether or not they believe they are leaving permanently. These could include birth certificates, passports, marriage certificate, benefit books, rent book, mortgage certificate and so on. If they are staying with the abuser, suggest that they keep a record of what is happening (possibly giving a copy to a solicitor), work out escape routes from different parts of the house, keep emergency numbers on the memory of the phone, teach children how to call for help safely, pack a bag of clothes and documents to keep at a friend's house and carry out other safety planning (see above).

## HELPING NON-ABUSING PARENTS TALK TO THEIR CHILDREN

For most women experiencing domestic violence, the children are the reason she stays with, leaves, or goes back to her abuser. They are almost always her highest priority throughout these processes. Some women find that talking to their children about what has happened and what is going to happen next is difficult and they need some suggestions on how to go about this. Many have little confidence in themselves or their parenting skills after constant undermining by the abuser. It is therefore important to give a survivor as much confidence as possible and to reassure her that she is the expert regarding her children. Tell her that children often do know what is going on and prefer to talk about it (Mullender *et al.*, forthcoming).

The following are possible questions to ask the woman as a way of starting off the discussion. They allow you both to start from her perspective on what the difficulties may be, and also to cover some of the ways she might communicate with her children.

- How much do your children already know about the violence? About why you are living in a refuge? About the men's programme their dad is on? About why they are going to court? About why dad has been arrested or sent to prison?
- What do you think they feel about what has been happening to you?
- Have you talked to any of them? Do you want to tell me about that?
- What are your anxieties or concerns about your children?
- What help or information do you want from me?

The following questions are suggestions for women to use to start a conversation with one or more of their children about the violence or about what will happen next.

- Do you know why we are living in a refuge/why we had to leave home/why I had to ask dad to leave home/why dad is on this programme?
- Do you want to tell me how you feel about it?
- Is there anything worrying you about it? Anything scary? Do you want to tell me about it?
- Can you draw me a picture of our new house? Can you draw me a picture of you and me in it?
- Can you draw me a picture of our family?
- Is there anyone in the family that you miss especially? Do you want to write to them or ring them up (if safe and possible).
- Do you feel OK about going to see dad on contact visits? (Or, if appropriate) how do you feel about not going to see dad for a while, perhaps for a long while?
- Is there anything that you would like us to do as a family this weekend?
- How are things at school?

Information and issues to cover with the woman.

- Local sources of appropriate counselling or other support services for children and young people.
- Local leisure and other facilities for children and young people who have moved to a new area, or help with finding out about these.
- Where she can get support for herself regarding issues relating to her children – has she kept in contact with anyone from the refuge or does she have trusted friends or relatives she can talk to?
- What support she might be able to expect from social services or family centres. This may include help getting nursery or playgroup places, assistance with furnishing a new home and with other practical matters, as well as emotional support and help in dealing with problems with children.
- How much she feels it is necessary to tell her children.
- The possibility that her children may know more than she thinks and be confused or distressed.
- That this isn't her fault and that you know and understand how it might make her feel to have to consider this.
- That witnessing violence as a child doesn't mean that her children are more likely to grow up to be violent or victims themselves.
- Different ways of communicating with children about their feelings – having a chat while doing something together or walking to the park might be better than making the situation artificial, which might make them feel that they are being told off. Some children, particularly young children, might prefer to draw or paint what they feel or how they see their new life, which often helps both the children and their mother see change in a positive way.

Information and issues for the woman to cover with her children include the facts that:

- violence is wrong and no one deserves it;
- it is not their fault and they are not to blame;
- their dad still loves them (if this is true) and that they can still see him when they want to, providing it is safe (again, if this is true);  ⮞

- their dad wants to change (if this is true) and that, even if he and mum never live together again, this is a good thing for him to be doing – it shows that he is taking responsibility for what he has done;
- their dad is still a risk to her safety and that this means they may have to do some things that may be difficult or annoying, or that they may not be able to do some things that they want to do, but they hope not for long. That she knows this isn't fair and that they will find a way to manage and enjoy being a family without any violence in it;
- having a violent dad doesn't mean that they are going to turn out violent, nor does it excuse them if they use violence.

POSSIBLE SOURCES OF FURTHER SUPPORT FOR WOMEN AND CHILDREN

The following are all services or forms of assistance that you may be able to suggest, provide, help to obtain, or give the woman information about that will help her children and herself:

- family and friends – even if they are far away, by post or phone;
- social services – 'children in need' services as well as child protection;
- family centres;
- youth services;
- education welfare services;
- support or help with getting re-housed;
- benefits offices – for example, for Community Care Grants for furnishing a new house;
- talking to the child's teacher or relevant member of the school staff;
- arranging somewhere safe for contact handover to take place;
- arranging somewhere appropriate for older children to do homework if they are living in temporary accommodation (homework clubs);
- after-school care, possibly via the school.

## CONCLUSION

Although domestic violence presents risks to the survivors, their children, their families and friends and the professionals working with them, there is a range of measures for dealing with these risks. These include legal remedies that the woman experiencing domestic violence can instigate, the use of formal child protection procedures (as described in Chapter 3), working with the woman on practical aspects of safety planning, giving the woman time, space and support to talk about her experiences if this is appropriate, helping her with communicating with her children and offering practical and other services for her children and for herself, particularly if they have to move to another area to escape the violence. Social workers may not always be the most appropriate people to provide all of these services but they will need to ensure that the needs of survivors of domestic violence are met in any child protection work that they are undertaking with specific children. They can also be a valuable and crucial starting point for women who are seeking help themselves.

---

**Case Study – Part 4**

Carla's mum, Jo, brings Sally home while Steve is out at work. Jo sits and talks to Teresa, helping her think what on earth she can do now. Then Jo remembers she has seen a helpline poster at the community centre where she does some part-time cleaning. That afternoon, she dials the number for Teresa, whose hands are shaking too much, and a really helpful woman talks to Teresa about the choices she has. She tells Teresa that it is not her fault she has been abused, that Steve has committed a crime and, amazingly, that there is help available. Apparently, these dreadful things happen to lots of women and there is a refuge in the next town where Teresa could go with the kids and be safe. She had never realised it was there. They would all have to share one room but there is a space free – which is a real bit of luck, it seems – and the woman would send someone to meet them at a pre-arranged place in town.

Teresa realises that she does not want to be in the house when Steve gets home. She is too scared of what he might do to her and the children. Fortunately, she has kept Sally off school because her face is all bruised and she hasn't been able to send Tommy today because no one got to sleep until the early hours and then they overslept. She bundles a few things for them all into a bag and they catch the bus into town. ➤

---

By early evening, they are in the refuge. It feels very strange, but a woman called a children's worker has taken Tommy to the playroom to meet some other children and Sally has made a friend called Linda, a year younger than herself. Teresa has had a good old cry and is now chatting with several of the other woman who have shown her the ropes and told her about their own experiences. Some of them are very similar to her own and she begins to think that, even if her world *has* just fallen in around her ears, at least it might not all be of her own making.

**Questions about the Case Study**

*1. As a social worker, could you have helped Teresa get the kind of support she has now received?*

*2. Would there have been any other safe options in this situation?*

# Direct work with children

**There is a major role which could be played by direct services aimed at helping children understand and recover from what they have experienced.**

At present, there is an acute shortage in the UK of group and individual help for children who have lived with domestic violence, and those who try to refer children for help are frequently confronted with either a lack of services or long waiting lists. Were family support to come more to the fore in social services' thinking (Department of Health, 1995), this would provide a framework within which such work could be routinely undertaken. Developments to date tend to have occurred in the voluntary sector, often on a piecemeal basis. Consequently, practice guidance stems largely from Canada and the USA.

The first step is for the practitioner to find out what is wrong in the child's life.

## HANDLING DISCLOSURES

Any trusted adult may be approached by a child who wants to talk about what is happening at home. Many of the skills in handling this (source for this section: *Making a Difference*, Children's Subcommittee of the London Coordinating Committee to End Woman Abuse, 1992) are identical to those practitioners would use in a disclosure of direct child abuse, including:

- noticing when the child is distressed and wants to talk;
- listening carefully;
- believing what the child is saying, no matter how far outside your own experience it may be.

If the child has not explicitly disclosed living with domestic violence:

- noticing when a child is experiencing some of the consequences listed in Chapter 3;
- being aware that these may be caused by domestic violence;
- using safe and appropriate methods to find out whether this is the case.

As with child abuse, too, an immediate concern must be whether the child is currently safe and, in the case of domestic violence, how you might find out whether his or her mother is safe or how you might safely get information to her about what help is available.

The manual *Making a Difference* offers age-related advice on safety planning with children.

The youngest children (pre-school) can learn:

- how to make an emergency telephone call;
- how to give their full name and address;
- what to say ('*Someone is hurting my mummy*' may be treated more urgently than '*My daddy is hurting my mummy*');
- who it is safe to run to; or
- where they can safely hide in the house;
- why it is not safe to try and help their mother.

The child's mother needs to know where her child will run to and who he or she will call in an emergency. Safety planning needs to be carried out in partnership with her.

Primary-school age children are very likely to believe the abuse is their fault. Handling a disclosure from a child of this age involves helping the child deal with his or her feelings as well as with the actual events and with safety issues as above. Children can be helped to understand:

- that they are not responsible for what is happening;
- that it is OK and normal to be very scared;
- what help you, as a professional, can give to deal with this;
- what you can and can't keep secret;
- that it would be safe to confide in you again.

As the manual states (p.228):

> Your goal is to make the child feel supported and safe... Give the child reassurance:
>
> *"I'm glad you told me; you did the right thing." "It's not your fault."*

Where adolescents are concerned, working out what they feel about the abuser and the abused woman will be a preoccupation, linked to thinking about their own boyfriends and girlfriends. This is an age-group where it may be particularly important to help them understand the dangers of intervening, concentrating instead on ensuring that they and any younger brothers and sisters go somewhere safe and on calling the police if possible. A young person may find it useful to talk about:

- the changing social attitudes to domestic violence;
- the fact that it is a crime;
- no one having the right to abuse another person;
- the specialist agencies they could contact for themselves;
- the agencies their mother might find helpful.

Broader discussion on anti-sexist attitudes and non-violent relationships can reassure young people that they have choices in their own lives.

At all ages, all the standard communication skills with children and young people provide the foundation for this disclosure work but the practitioner needs, in addition, to develop some specialist knowledge. This includes learning about the forms that domestic abuse takes – so as not to frighten the child or young person away by being shocked or disbelieving – and knowing what channels of help are available locally. When children start trying to talk about what is going on at home, they can be asked sensitive but direct questions that help tell their story. Practitioners who do not know how to offer such help while safeguarding confidentiality may unwittingly place children and their mothers at heightened risk.

## CHILDREN'S GROUPS

Groups are an ideal way of bringing children together so they know they are not alone in what they have experienced. There can be a tendency for parents and professionals to assume that children are unaffected if they do not talk about the violence. In fact, they may be keeping it bottled up inside, and parents may have been less successful in hiding the violence than they think. A group provides the ideal opportunity to talk about it (Mullender, 1994a).

Evaluation of children's groups in the USA and Canada has been encouraging:

- 92% of children and 87% of mothers/caregivers surveyed rated them positively (Loosley *et al*, 1997). Groups have also shown effective outcomes (Marshall *et al*, 1995; Peled and Edleson, 1995; Loosley *et al*, 1997).

They can:

- change children's mistaken views about their responsibility for the violence;
- teach them how to protect themselves and seek help safely;
- help them learn about abuse, non-violence and non-violent conflict resolution;
- be fun;
- build children's self-confidence;
- break the secret about the violence at home.

There are useful manuals available on how to run a group (Peled and Davis, 1995; Loosley *et al*, 1997).

A pre-group interview, often at home or at the shelter (refuge), introduces the groupworkers to the child and his or her carer and family circumstances. It helps the worker to know that the child is:

- acknowledging that there has been abuse in the home;
- ready to talk about it (or to listen thoughtfully);
- able to do so safely.

If the danger is still current, group membership may be postponed or, if the child is currently very distressed, other help may be offered. The child does not have to be clear about the seriousness of, or responsibility for, the abuse; the group will offer the chance to work on these issues.

This interview helps the child to understand that:

- it is OK to talk to these strangers about the violence;
- there is a choice whether or not to join the group;
- it will be a group where all the children have seen their mothers abused and where some of them have been abused too;
- group members will talk about what happened and how they felt;
  but
- no one will be forced to say anything they don't want to;
- it is OK still to love your father or stepfather but to *'dislike what he does that hurts others'*

**(Loosley *et al*, 1997, p.15)**

SOME POINTERS ABOUT GROUPS

- Divide groups by age, with some flexibility according to developmental stage but normally only spanning 2 or 3 years' difference;
- children as young as 4 can be catered for, provided they are attending some form of day care or pre-school setting that has accustomed them to being in a group;
- there should normally be up to 6 younger children or up to 8 older children in a group;
- the groups should be closed;
- groups set their own ground rules, with 'confidentiality' and 'no violence' to the fore;
- most groups are mixed sex;
- groups normally run for 10 weeks (8 weeks for the youngest);
- they follow a programme of topics, using a range of age-related activities;
- they usually run weekly, but can be twice-weekly over half as many weeks, or even daily, in the summer holiday;
- sessions last for an hour and a half with refreshments halfway;
- facilitators can be two women or a woman and a man;  ▶

- at least one facilitator should be experienced in groupwork;
- at least one should be knowledgeable about domestic violence and its impact on children;
- all the usual groupwork practices of co-worker planning and debriefing, recording and evaluating apply;
- not only the group as a whole but individual participation should be monitored, with identification of child and family themes on which the referring agency may want to base further help.

## SUGGESTED CONTENT OF A GROUP

A brief outline of a standard, ten-week group is given below (drawn from Loosley *et al*, 1997). The first three sessions and the seventh, on safety planning, are essential, whatever other adaptations are made. All group sessions start and finish with 'check in' and 'check out': how the children's week has been and how they have felt about the group that week. This brings current experiences and feelings to the fore, and helps the groupworkers know what they are dealing with.

### WEEK 1

*Violence in the family. What violence is – physical, emotional and sexual abuse; that it is widespread throughout society and against women (and children) in families, and that it is wrong. Awareness-raising that all types of abuse – physical, emotional, and sexual are equally hurtful, damaging and unacceptable.*

### WEEK 2

*Identifying and understanding feelings. Feeling something different on the outside (often anger) and on the inside (for example, sad, scared, jealous, embarrassed). Emotions in daily life and their purpose.*

### WEEK 3

*Talking about the violence. Video or TV clip leading into talking about the children's own experiences, with the youngest ones drawing a picture of this and showing it to the group.*

## WEEK 4

*Anger and conflict resolution. Alternative solutions that are safe, fair and workable, and how they would make people feel. The youngest children play at pulling angry faces and build an erupting volcano together to illustrate bottled-up feelings (use baking powder, food colouring and washing-up liquid!). Teenagers spend more time discussing taking responsibility and peer accountability.*

## WEEK 5

*Responsibility for violence and abuse lying with the perpetrator, not with the woman or the children. Exploding myths about woman abuse. A children's version of the power and control wheel is developed, with children and young people filling in blank segments with their own experiences.*

## WEEK 6

*Family changes as a result of violence, for example, parents separating, mother and children leaving home (perhaps several times), changing schools. Things they miss the most; best and worst things.*

## WEEK 7

*Safety planning. How to be safe and not involve themselves in the violence, somewhere safe to go if it happens, how to call the police (if it's safe to get to the phone), talking to a trusted adult.*

## WEEK 8

*Sexual abuse prevention. The teenage session also covers dating violence.*

## WEEK 9

*Self-esteem and feelings of self-worth. (Also, beginning to prepare for the end of the group and planning the final session.) Accepting praise from others, making posters about themselves.*

## WEEK 10

*Closure. Feelings about the group, what it has done, what has been learnt. Telling the world about ending*

*violence. Final celebration (for example, a pizza party).
Special things the groupworkers will remember about
each child in the group, closing ceremony with a candle
you can still see in your head with your eyes closed (that
is, remembering the group) and then blown out together.*

*After the group finishes, a post-group interview picks
up issues from the group that may need to be taken
forward for further help and also provides the family's
feedback on the group.*

### NEED FOR FLEXIBILITY

Group sessions should be varied where particular needs
arise in the group, for example, one group of 8 to 10 year
olds were mainly speaking about their experiences for the
first time and needed several sessions before they could
move on. A group of teenagers needed to work on personal
safety and forms of help available in abusive dating
relationships. Content varies to some extent in any group
according to the particular needs of members and creativity
of the groupworkers. Younger children tend to respond to
more activity and less talking. So, for example, answers to:
*'Where do you see violence?'* might be drawn on Post-It
notes by the workers (TV set, children's playground) and
stuck on flip-chart paper by the youngest children, or
drawn for themselves by those slightly older, or written up
on a flip-chart by teenagers and then discussed.

### PARALLEL WORK WITH MOTHERS

Most groups are for children only. A few involve mothers
in the same group or in a parallel one that shares the last
couple of sessions (Peled and Edleson, 1995). The parent-
child groups are useful for families that are re-forming
with the woman as head of the household. Topics which
can be covered in this context include:

- setting non-violent boundaries for children's behaviour;
- safe ways of talking together about what have been family secrets;
- disclosing other secrets (for example, direct child abuse);
- comparing memories of traumatic events (of which children may know more than their parents think, yet may have an incomplete knowledge or understanding); ▶

- establishing a more open pattern of communication for the future;
- seeing themselves as survivors who can create a non-violent future together.

Whatever model is chosen, mothers need to know the content so that they can understand and support their children's group experiences, whilst also respecting the group's confidentiality.

Groups are springing up in the UK, usually run by one of the national children's charities. Children's meetings and workshops in refuges also cover some of the same issues and help to empower children while living there.

## CHILDREN'S COUNSELLING SERVICES

An alternative to groupwork is to offer children an individual opportunity to talk about their experiences and to come to terms with them, arriving at a better understanding of who is to blame and what might happen in the future. This may also be a better option:

- where the child is currently too distressed to settle into a group;
- where commitment to group attendance is unrealistic owing to continuing danger and the likelihood of further unplanned moves;
- where there is no group available.

All practitioners who offer individual help to children need to know the impact that living with domestic violence can have and the issues to which it gives rise. At present, such expertise is rarely available to children, even when they are referred for help as children exhibiting problems rather than as 'problem' children. Those who need the right knowledge and skills to work with children on these issues include:

- child psychologists;
- child psychiatrists;
- social workers in child protection and in children's and families' teams;
- residential social workers;

- alcohol and drugs teams working with young people;
- youth offending teams;
- education social workers;
- primary health care workers;
- hospital staff in children's settings.

Medical and other staff can often find themselves dealing with symptoms that are apparently resistant to treatment or intervention because they are actually a reaction to home circumstances. These can include eating and sleeping disorders in children who are too young to explain what the matter is, as well as young people's offending, running away, or escaping into drugs.

In the UK, the only nationwide expertise in working with children living with domestic violence and its aftermath is located amongst children's workers in women's refuges. Many of them offer what they call 'one-to-one work', that is, structured time with individual children when they can talk about whatever is on their mind. In some refuges, a fixed time is set aside (such as after the weekly children's meeting) when the children's worker will be available (Mullender et al, 1998). It is a natural reaction to show distress as a result of living with violence and children can gain enormous emotional support from being able to talk about it, including through play activities.

Although refuge workers do not offer in-depth therapy, they have always been trusted with disclosures of child abuse, including child sexual abuse which they helped reveal as an endemic problem in society. Refuges have always been a safe place where children may find themselves able to talk about their abuse for the first time. One refuge worker was being approached so often for advice by local social workers, that she eventually worked with them, and with the local branch of a national children's charity, to establish a specialist resource solely for sexual abuse survivors. It is important for other professionals to respect what child workers in refuges offer children (Hague et al, 1996), including through outreach and aftercare work. An evaluation for the National Council of Voluntary Child Care Organisations

(Ball, 1990) called for local government to fund one children's worker for every 6 adult beds available in women's refuges, but many are still forced to depend on part-time and volunteer help. Social services could play a much bigger role in recognising this work.

Beyond the refuge movement there is little in the way of a specialist response to individual children who have lived with domestic violence. One children's counselling service that has been established is run by Warwickshire Domestic Violence Support Services (contactable at 37a, Regent Street, Rugby CV21 2PE). It aims to work with children who are past the stage of immediate danger and who have issues they are now ready to work on.

---

**Case study – Part 5**

It is now some time later and Teresa and the children have been rehoused. Tommy starts going to the children's group at the local family centre. He is with 6 other children within a year or so of his own age and is amazed to find that their dads and stepdads have all hit their mums like his has. He has always thought he is the only one because it has been such a big secret. At the first meeting, they all draw pictures to show why they think they have come to the group. Tommy draws a big fist in the middle of the page and colours it pink. There are sticking-out lines and clouds of dust all round it to show it is moving in for a punch, like on the Saturday morning TV cartoons. He has also seen a poster at the library about people hitting each other but he thinks his drawing is a lot better. Everyone else says it is good, too, which he really likes. At home, he has mostly been getting told off and at school he is frightened of one of the bigger boys – so it makes a change to get something right and be treated nicely. Halfway through the group there is a break for juice and biscuits. The grown-ups are called Hilary and Jim – they never say *'Don't be so silly'* when the kids talk about stuff at home like most people do. Jim gets the juice out and puts it away, which surprises Tommy because Steve never used to fetch anything at home. This group is going to be full of surprises, by the look of it.

At the group, he makes a new friend called Sam who is also frightened of his dad, and together they make a plasticine animal called 'Big Scary Monster' that can come in the night and frighten off anyone who gets in their dreams and wakes them up.

Sally has also found people to talk to. She has been going back to the refuge, sometimes on a Tuesday evening when there is an 'open house' for teenagers who have been through the refuge. She always makes sure she gets there early because Marie, one of the workers, makes time to have a coffee and ask her how she is. Sally still feels confused about everything that has happened. She can't understand how her mum could have stayed with Steve after he started hitting  ➤

---

◄ her, or why so many women in the refuge go back to their blokes. Don't the workers get fed up with it? Marie explains all the reasons why it's hard for women to make a new life for themselves and their children, and that many of them are still very scared of the men who have hit them, as well as often still loving them. Sally thinks this makes it sound very difficult to find a boyfriend who will love and respect you, and makes her mind up never to let a boy get the better of her.

Sally knows Marie will understand anything, even really difficult things about people and feelings and worrying about it all and so on. So, eventually, Sally is able to tell Marie the very worst secret she has been keeping about Steve and her mum: that time he hit her and hit her and then forced her to have sex on the kitchen floor, with his hand over her mouth to stop her screaming. Absolutely no one knows that Sally saw this but she had to get up to go to the toilet and was on the landing when it happened, too terrified to move. The kitchen door was open and she couldn't help looking, though she quickly hid her face. Was she a pervert for watching even a bit of it? Why wouldn't her legs move to run down and kick Steve off her mum? Had her mum wanted it to happen and did that mean she was a slag? Afterwards, Sally was sick in the toilet, then washed her face and went back to bed. She couldn't talk to her mum about it, obviously, and who could you tell about a thing like that?

It is the biggest relief in the world to tell Marie. Then Marie hugs her and tells her it's all right, and that there wouldn't have been anything she could have done, and that what Steve did was wrong and was part of the reason he was in trouble with the police, and that no man has a right to treat any woman like that and that it doesn't mean the woman is bad. It was part of her being abused, like the hitting, and that is why there are refuges and other ways now of helping women and children. Sally has done the right thing to talk about it and she can come and talk to Marie again, any time she wants. Would she like Marie to come round to talk quietly to her and her mum, sometime when Tommy is out? Would Sally feel better if she could tell her mum that she knows what happened to her? Maybe it would even help. Her mum might feel less guilty if Sally can tell her she understands why they had to leave home.

---

**Questions about the Case Study**

*1. What opportunities are there in your agency to offer direct services to children who have lived with domestic violence?*

*2. What other agencies could be approached to take on this work and how could it be funded?*

*3. What will happen to children and young people like Tommy and Sally if they don't get help to sort out their feelings and their understandings of what has happened?*

*4. What kinds of services do you think would help them most?*

# Prevention and effective co-ordination

**Whenever we help a woman and her children to be safe, we are working preventively. There are three levels of prevention to think about. These are:**

**primary**
preventing domestic abuse from happening in the first place;

**secondary**
preventing its recurrence once an agency learns it is happening;

**tertiary**
preventing the worst of the impact on those who have already experienced it (a kind of damage limitation).

## PRIMARY PREVENTION (PREVENTING DOMESTIC VIOLENCE FROM HAPPENING AT ALL)

### PUBLIC EDUCATION
Zero Tolerance campaigns target the general public with a message that all forms of woman and child abuse constitute criminal behaviour and will no longer be condoned. An evaluation of the original campaign by the then Edinburgh District Council (Foley, 1993) reported that women found it an empowering experience to see men challenged to take responsibility for their behaviour. It is also supportive for practitioners to have their work underpinned by a comprehensive anti-violence stance in their local authority.

### WORK IN SCHOOLS
The reason for intervening early with children is not to 'break the cycle' ('cycle of abuse' theories have been highly contentious in relation to domestic violence – see Widom,

1989; Morley and Mullender, 1994) but to assist all children to grow up with healthy attitudes and to offer particular help to those currently living with violence. Schools can choose one of several ways to teach children what domestic violence is and to point out that it is wrong.

- Ideally, work on non-violent relationships in school, family and community should be integrated into the mainstream curriculum, for example in PHSE (personal, health and social education);
- there has been great success in Canada and the USA with designating a special violence-awareness week encompassing the whole curriculum (Mullender, 1994b; Gamache and Snapp, 1995; Sudermann et al, 1995), with the local media and the entire home-school community also joining in;
- school-based work on bullying, already widespread, can provide a useful channel into wider non-violence work encompassing violence against women, child abuse, and racist and homophobic attacks. Childworkers from refuges not infrequently work with schools on all these issues (Hague et al, 1996).

There is now a lot of educational material available, including:

- Islington's STOP pack (London Borough of Islington, 1995b);
- Hackney's RESPECT educational pack for primary and secondary schools (Hackney Council, not dated);
- Guidance for Schools, produced in Leeds (Leeds City Council Education Department and Leeds Inter-Agency Project, not dated);
- Northamptonshire's Relationships Without Fear (Northamptonshire County Council, not dated).

Any work of this kind needs considerable preparation. Teachers need training and support to handle disclosures of direct and indirect abuse appropriately (see previous chapter – Direct work with children). Links with social services and relevant women's groups need strengthening beforehand, so that referrals can be well handled and increased levels of work dealt with.

### YOUTH SERVICES AND LEISURE SERVICES

Young people's awareness of domestic violence as a crime can also be raised through leisure activities. This can help them learn to support one another, and find out what additional help is available and from where. In Fife, for example, there has been extensive work with young people on violence against women and children spearheaded from within the local authority; a youth conference (Fife Zero Tolerance Campaign, 1996) sought funding under the auspices of the UN Declaration on the Rights of the Child which accords children and young people the right to be heard on issues that affect them.

Libraries have a self-evidently important role to play in public education. They can:

> ● stock books for children and adults that provide up-to-date information about domestic violence and what can be done about it;
> ● display posters and leaflets about confidential sources of help;
> ● display Zero Tolerance or other local authority campaign materials on the issue.

Leisure services more generally can become involved through film, theatre, talks and discussions.

### OTHER POSSIBILITIES

Health promotion and crime prevention are amongst other services which could be tapped in local areas to pursue primary prevention agendas.

## SECONDARY PREVENTION (PREVENTING REPEAT ATTACKS)

The key issue here, for professionals in all practice settings, is to recognise domestic violence when it is presented to them and to intervene in ways which are of positive assistance to women and children.

### EMERGENCY SERVICES FOR ABUSED WOMEN AND CHILDREN

At the top of any list of services aimed at stopping domestic violence at the earliest possible moment – and certainly as soon as a woman feels able to ask for help – must come the independent, emergency help offered by

Women's Aid and other women's organisations.

The Women's Aid ethos *empowers women* to take control of their own and their children's lives. Workers and volunteers, often themselves survivors of abuse, provide support and advice on housing, legal and benefits issues. As well as *emergency accommodation and halfway houses*, many refuge projects also provide *outreach and advocacy services*, not only for women and children while they are in the refuge, but also for many still living with the violence or who are trying to rebuild their lives elsewhere.

Refuges are the best-known service for abused women. They provide safe emergency accommodation for women and children fleeing domestic violence.

- There are two hundred and fifty refuges affiliated to the Women's Aid Federation of England (WAFE).
- In 1996/7, they made 54,500 admissions, including over 32,000 children, and
- responded to an estimated 145,000 telephone calls (WAFE, 1998).

Yet Britain lacks a long-term funding strategy for refuges; demand always exceeds supply. There are Women's Aid federations also in Wales, Scotland and Northern Ireland, as well as other refuges run independently. Specialist refuges support many ethnic minority women and children. Women do not need to be referred to a refuge – they can make their own contact. It is vitally important, however, that every practitioner knows how to help a woman ring the national Women's Aid national helpline or their local Women's Aid group.

National co-ordination helps women move around the country to find a vacancy in an area where they hope they will not be traced. Some women have to move several times when their abusers track them down. This is why it is crucial that practitioners *never, under any circumstances, reveal the whereabouts of a woman or child escaping violence* to a man or his representative – including his solicitor. Even revealing that you know where she is may put both you and the woman in danger.

## WHAT ABOUT THE MEN? THE CRIMINAL AND CIVIL JUSTICE RESPONSE

Despite an official expectation that domestic attacks
should now be treated as seriously as any other form of
violent crime, there are numerous problems in the current
operation of the law and the courts:

- rates of arrest are still too low;
- the Crown Prosecution Service is notorious for dropping and
  downgrading charges;
- sentences are frequently too light.

There are problems, too, for women in gaining access to
the courts, including:

- reductions in legal aid entitlement;
- a lack of legal redress against psychological abuse
  (Yearnshire, 1996);
- yet the onus is almost always on the woman to pursue her
  case through the courts, despite the danger of retaliation from
  her abuser.

There is currently growing interest in personal alarm
schemes for women, operated either by the police or
through extensions of local authority systems for older
people. Because the alarms have been introduced in a
piecemeal fashion and were never intended for this
particular use, there tend to be:

- no eligibility criteria;
- too few available (especially for longer term use);
- risks inherent in the equipment being visible to the abuser;
- reliance on a telephone connection which is easily cut by
  him.

Though they can help in some circumstances, alarms are
no alternative to effective action against abusive men.

The main method used to try and change the attitudes
and behaviour of abusive men is groupwork (Morran and
Wilson, 1997). Any practitioner considering referring a

man to a group needs to find out certain things about it (Mullender, 1996, chapter nine):

- First, only some groups run to a *model based on a clear recognition of domestic violence as a crime*. Anger management, for example, is not an appropriate response because domestic violence rests on abusive men's belief system about male/female relationships, not on how they manage their emotions. Consequently, it needs a re-educational, not a therapeutic approach.
- Second, there is a need for *long-term evaluation* of individual outcomes, with feedback from the woman, not just the man. He may claim to have changed in order to persuade his partner to stay or return home. In fact, drop-out rates are high and improvement may be short-lived or superficial. Claims to change men's behaviour that don't work may be more dangerous than doing nothing because they open up renewed opportunities to abuse.
- Third, and most importantly, *the safety of women and children must be paramount*. The groupworkers need to have a channel for learning instantly if the woman or the children are revictimised by the man, as well as receiving routine feedback from her about the man's progress. He can then be challenged in the group if necessary.

Accountability to women more generally is also an issue in work with men. It includes:

- not competing for resources with services for women and children (currently being cut in many parts of the country);
- involving women as co-workers, consultants and committee members to ensure that any men involved in running the programme do not begin to collude with the abusers;
- Some forms of men's groups may minimise or decriminalise domestic violence in comparison with other violent crime (Burton *et al*, 1998). If the man's attendance is voluntary he may well drop out when the going gets tough. Court-mandated attendance at least builds in sanctions. Diversion from sentencing is criticised for not making men take responsibility for the impact of their crimes.

A checklist of essential minimum standards for men's programmes is available from the Domestic Violence Intervention Project (PO Box 2838, London W6 9ZE).

## MEN AS FATHERS

Although it only makes sense against a background of comprehensive services to tackle the fundamental problem of men's violence, there is also work in the USA designed to promote violent men's awareness of their responsibilities as fathers (Mathews, 1995), including in the African American community (Williams, 1994). This involves focusing on the impact of their behaviour on their children and teaching non-violent parenting skills, together with knowledge of child development. Key features include the need to work with men's resistance and shame, while harnessing their genuine feelings for their children. Sometimes, men are court-mandated to attend such a programme. Though there is current UK debate on requiring men to take fathering more seriously, their dangerousness has to be tackled first (Farmer and Owen, 1995; Hester and Radford, 1996) before finding ways of involving them more in child care contexts (Milner, 1993).

## TERTIARY PREVENTION (HARM REDUCTION)

Once a woman or a child has lived with domestic violence, there can be far-reaching consequences which, in themselves, deserve intervention to stop the damage going any further. Although this is an area in which social workers have particular skills, it is not one in which they have been encouraged to invest time and many of the services that could be most helpful to women and children (women's groups, children' groups, specialist counselling services) are underdeveloped or absent in most parts of Britain. The projects that do exist tend to be in the voluntary sector and chronically overstretched, though some are excellent.

Improved responses right across public sector services could assist abused women and their children to rebuild shattered lives. Many find themselves living in poverty and effectively homeless, though not always able to convince the housing authorities of this. Deficiencies in health, justice and social work responses have already been noted. In addition, some young people leave home and live on the streets in preference to remaining in a situation where they or their mothers are being abused; others find their schooling disrupted by the impact of the abuse on their physical or emotional well-being or by constant moves – this may lead to truancy, school exclusion or lack of educational attainment. There is an urgent need for raised awareness in the education and youth offending services of the impact of living with domestic violence and direct abuse.

All these preventive efforts, when in place, need to be co-ordinated across whole local authorities and inter-agency groupings.

## CO-ORDINATING STRATEGIES FOR TACKLING DOMESTIC VIOLENCE

### ESTABLISHING AN AUTHORITY-WIDE POLICY

Every local authority needs to take its own policy stand on the issue of domestic violence (Mullender and Humphreys with Saunders, 1998). Only through co-ordinated, strategic planning, within and beyond each authority, will efforts have the maximum impact. Links with wider equalities policies are needed to ensure that the needs of all sections of the local population are met, since domestic violence occurs in all communities and to all types of women.

Good practice guidelines can either be issued on an authority-wide or department-specific basis. They aim to make practitioners aware of the difficulties and dangers facing women and children seeking help and of how they can best respond to these (see, for example, London Borough of Islington, 1995a). Some of the elements stressed in such guides are:

The utmost tact and sensitivity are required, over and above the normal good practice issues, such as:

- *confidentiality* as a major safety issue;
- the importance of *not forming judgements against women* who choose to stay or to return home;
- *no prerequisites for offering help* such as the pursuit of a particular course of action or the production of proof of abuse; ▶

- *working with the woman's choice*, according to what she judges to be safe and right for her and her children;
- *understanding the dangers* involved in an abused woman even asking for help, given the fear of repercussions from her abuser and the possible effect on her self-esteem of prolonged verbal and emotional abuse;
- having the *option of a woman staff member* to speak to wherever possible;
- understanding that *many women fear losing their children* if they approach social services for help;
- women whose *residence status* in the UK is in question (especially those who have lived here for less than twelve months) have an additional reason to fear 'official' intervention.

Other specific measures which can help make a local authority response more effective include:

- having *interpreters* readily available;
- opportunities for *children to be safely occupied* while the woman is being interviewed about intimate and distressing matters.

### DOMESTIC VIOLENCE INTER-AGENCY FORUMS

Forums can work on a range of issues:

- *recording cases* involving domestic violence under a separate category so that involvement can be monitored, resources argued for and outcomes measured;
- designating a *specialist post or team*;
- developing a comprehensive training strategy (see Hester *et al*, 1998a and 1998b for useful materials) and
- building *domestic violence into staff care and staff safety policies*, both in relation to tackling abusive men and in assisting individual employees who are facing current danger from violence in their own lives. Examples of practical measures can include blocking telephone calls to the workplace from an abuser, alerting reception staff, and agreeing to a change of workplace where requested.

There are now over two hundred domestic violence forums in the UK (Hague and Malos, 1996; Malos *et al*, 1996). What can help them work?

- Fostering inter-agency co-operation;
- public education;
- developing new services;
- making existing services more responsive to the needs of women and children who live with abuse;
- Some forums have sub-groups specifically to look at issues for children.

## AREA CHILD PROTECTION COMMITTEES

- Some of the most successful ACPCs employ *designated workers* to hold all the threads together and maintain the momentum of change from meeting to meeting; this avoids the risk of becoming just a 'talking shop'.
- Forums need their own *policy statements and good practice guidelines to establish a shared philosophy* about domestic violence, its causes and the appropriate responses.
- They also need an *appropriate level of representation* from member agencies to take decisions and allocate resources. Ironically, those local authority departments whose staff are amongst the most heavily involved with abused women and their children – social services, housing and education – are sometimes amongst the least involved in their local forum, or do not send people with a broad enough remit or sufficient authority to effect change.
- Effective partnership means that *power differences between statutory and voluntary agencies need to be overcome*. Local authorities need to avoid duplicating, appropriating, undermining or seeking to control the work of voluntary bodies.
- At the same time, ways need to be found of directly or indirectly *hearing the voice of women and children* who have experienced domestic violence, so as to ensure that activities relate directly to their needs and experiences, with their *safety as the paramount consideration.*

> ◀
> ● In particular, strategies to *raise the profile of Women's Aid and of black women's groups* are important and need appropriate resourcing.

The Area Child Protection Committee (ACPC) is an already existing inter-agency grouping that can play a key role. Indeed, in some areas, the ACPC has taken the lead on strategic planning and guidance for children's issues in relation to domestic violence. Through drawing together representatives from health, education, the police, the NSPCC, social services, women's refuges, and the local domestic violence forum, Cleveland ACPC, for example, produced a policy statement and a practice guidance booklet (Cleveland ACPC, 1995). Other ACPCs have produced similar practice guidelines for inter-agency co-operation and have mounted multidisciplinary conferences. There is a clear need for formalised co-ordination between the ACPC and any local domestic violence forums to avoid duplication of effort or pulling in different directions.

### CHILDREN'S SERVICES PLANS

Children's Services Plans are a requirement for social service authorities. They provide a real chance to commit the local authority and associated agencies to future service provision for children living with domestic violence, for example by recognising them as 'children in need' under the Children Act 1989. This means that s.17 money can then be used for family support and direct services, which may save on s.47 child protection involvement in the longer term. The Department of Health (1996) has made clear that there is a health service role in assisting local authorities in identifying children in need; health professionals therefore need the same raised awareness of domestic violence as do social workers and other relevant professsionals (BMA, 1998). The Plans also offer an opportunity to alter the balance between family support services and child protection investigations (Department of Health, 1995) since effective support to both women and children can often keep them together in safety.

### COMMUNITY SAFETY PLANS

A crime audit by each local authority is now a required part of its crime reduction strategy, and we need to ensure that it covers domestic violence. The resulting Community Safety Plans provide an excellent opportunity to get all parts of the criminal and civil justice system working together with local authorities, the voluntary sector and health professionals to work more effectively for women and children's safety and to tackle the behaviour of men. All the problems with policing and prosecuting domestic violence which were outlined above could be tackled through this channel.

### COMMUNITY CARE PLANS

Community Care Plans may seem less relevant to children but mothers who are experiencing domestic violence may themselves present to any of the adult services or to any health care setting and this may provide an opening to meet their and their children's needs. These Plans are also the only place where local authorities can record their intentions to provide or support services designated specifically for women, as opposed to their children.

### CONCLUSION

Inadequate provision, or no provision at all, in the sphere of domestic violence is no longer publicly acceptable. There is widespread support for public education campaigns pointing out that domestic violence, like other forms of abuse of women and children, is a crime and will no longer be condoned. Strategic planning, within and across relevant agencies, needs to incorporate properly thought-out policies on tackling such abuse and dealing sensitively with its aftermath.

## Case study – Part 6

Steve Bennett is taken by his probation officer to meet one of the facilitators of the men's group he has been told about. It sounds quite tough. There are rules to follow and he will be expected to talk very honestly about what he has done to Teresa and Sally, as well as the effect it has had on Tommy. A woman worker will be asking Teresa from time to time how Steve is treating her and, if he hits her again, he could be asked to leave the group and be taken back to court. Steve still isn't quite sure whether he belongs with hardened criminals who have been beating their wives up for years. People are putting all the blame on him, but Teresa does nag so and Sally will get herself into trouble if someone doesn't stop her. But he does want to try and save his marriage so he signs the agreement to attend the group regularly and stick to its rules.

Teresa is feeling a whole lot better now she knows she can ring the Women's Aid outreach worker whenever she needs to. Getting the help for the children,too, means that she has more time to think about her own feelings. She still loves Steve but can she ever trust him again? Those things he said to the social worker about her not being a fit mother to the twins! She knows, deep down, they're not true but Steve said so many awful things; it's hard to believe she's going to be able to cope on her own with four children. Would that 'return to study' course she saw advertised really be a possibility? She might go to the refuge drop-in this week and see what the others think.

Sally is looking forward to seeing the workers at the refuge this week. She wants to talk to them about whether her mum might take Steve back and whether she has been over-reacting in chucking her own boyfriend. He shoved her up against a wall at school, while they were arguing, and she got really scared that he was turning out to be like Steve. She has also had the idea of enlisting Marie's help with a project she wants to do at school as part of a 'Respecting ourselves and others' week. It's on 'Challenges facing women in the new millennium' and Sally reckons the refuge workers will have some good ideas because they have helped so many women make really big choices in their lives. She wants to write about jobs and marriage and kids and all sorts of things, and about how girls should be able to make their own minds up and boys should understand why that is important. She'll put pictures of the 'Spice Girls' in it, and write 'Girlpower' on the front. She has started thinking about being a social worker when she leaves school so she wants to get really good marks this year.

Tommy misses Steve quite a lot. Sally says he is too horrid to bother with because of what he has done to their mum but Tommy still wants to see him and tells his mum and the workers at the children's group so. After a bit, Steve starts coming round to take Tommy out on a Saturday afternoon but it isn't very nice when Steve comes to the house to fetch him because he yells at Tommy's mum and hits his fist on the door. He also kicks Tommy's new toy truck  ➤

◄◄ across the floor and breaks one of the wheels. Tommy hates it when Steve is like that because it makes him remember all the other times. Then he starts shaking and wants to run to his mum and hold on to her legs, or sit on her lap and hide his face. He wouldn't want his friends to know he still does that, but some days he still feels quite little despite being at proper school now. Pooch is also nice to cuddle up to, and Tommy is glad Steve didn't hurt the dog when he threatened to that time Tommy was naughty. Tommy knows from the group that it wasn't really his fault, though, and also that it is OK to feel sad and scared.

Teresa makes a mental note to remember to tell that probation woman how Steve turned a bit nasty when he came to take Tommy out at the weekend. They can have that out with him in the group. He is probably Mr Nice when he goes there – she is the only person who knows what he's really like. Only now she knows from chats at the refuge that, even though there are thousands of blokes like Steve, she and the kids don't have to put up with it and it's his responsibility, not theirs. The best thing was seeing that poster at the bus stop showing a man in quite a smart suit who had hit his wife. It all needs bringing out in the open. Then perhaps the social workers will believe women when they try to explain why they are too scared to do right by their kids some of the time. You'd think they'd know that, with all their training.

But then, domestic violence has been hushed up for so long. She should know – she's done enough in her time to stop people finding out and it's still embarrassing to talk about it to new people. It makes such a difference when you can tell from the way they talk to you that they understand why you didn't leave sooner, and don't look down on you as if it was all your fault for being a rotten wife. The probation office has a poster up about a helpline so you know the minute you walk in there that they understand what women go through.

But like that other poster said – Zero Tolerance. Never again. And with support from all the people who're now trying to help her and the kids, and even making Steve face up to what he has done – Who knows? It might come true.

---

**Questions about the Case Study**

*1.   Can violent men change?*

*2.   How can we avoid colluding with abusive men's denial and minimisation of what they have done and with unrealistic claims to have changed?*

*3.   In what ways can we demonstrate that we regard women and children as survivors, not as victims?*

*4.   What aftercare services need to be available for women and children?*

# Bibliography

Ball, M (1990) *Children's Workers in Women's Aid Refuges: a Report on the Experience of Nine Refuges in England* London; National Council of Voluntary Child Care Organisations.

BMA (British Medical Association) (1998) *Domestic Violence: a Health Care Issue?* London; BMA.

Burton, S, Regan, L and Kelly, L (1998) *Supporting Women and Challenging Men: Lessons from the Domestic Violence Intervention Project* Bristol: The Policy Press. (Based at the University of Bristol, 34 Tyndalls Park Road, Bristol BS8 1PY)

*Children Act* (1989) London; HMSO

Children's Subcommittee of the London Coordinating Committee to End Woman Abuse (1994) *Making a Difference* London, Ontario; Children's Aid Society of London and Middlesex.

Cleveland ACPC (Area Child Protection Committee) (1995) *ACPC Practice Guidance: Domestic Violence: Whose Problem Is It?* Middlesbrough; Cleveland ACPC.

Debbonaire, T (1998) *Responding with Respect: Meeting the Needs of Black Women Experiencing Domestic Violence in Hammersmith and Fulham* London; London Borough of Hammersmith and Fulham.

Department of Health (1995) *Child Protection: Messages from Research* London; HMSO.

Department of Health (1996) *Child Health in the Community* London; Department of Health.

Department of Health, Home Office, Department for Education and Employment, the National Assembly for Wales (1999) *Working Together to Safeguard Children: A Guide to Inter-Agency Working to Safeguard and Promote the Welfare of Children, Draft Consultation Paper* London; Department of Health.

Dobash, R E, Dobash, R P and Cavanagh, K (1985) 'The contact between battered women and social and medical agencies' in Pahl, J *Private Violence and Public Policy: The Needs of Battered Women and the Response of the Public Services* London; Routledge and Kegan Paul.

*Family Law Act* (1996) London; HMSO.

Farmer, E and Owen, M (1995) *Child Protection Practice: Private Risks and Public Remedies* London; HMSO.

Fife Zero Tolerance Campaign (1996) *Voices of the Future* Auchterderran: The Zero Tolerance Campaign in Fife.

Foley, R (1993) 'Zero Tolerance' *Trouble and Strife* 27, Winter, pp.16–20.

Forman, J (1995) *Is There a Correlation between Child Sexual Abuse and Domestic Violence? An Exploratory Study of the Links between Child Sexual Abuse and Domestic Violence in a Sample of Intrafamilial Child Sexual Abuse Cases*, Glasgow; Women's Support Project (Lawson's Building, 1700 London Road, Glasgow G32 8XD; reprint of an earlier, undated report).

Gamache, D and Snapp, S (1995) 'Teach your children well: elementary schools and violence prevention' in Peled, E, Jaffe, P G and Edleson, J L (1995) *Ending the Cycle of Violence: Community Responses to Children of Battered Women* Thousand Oaks, California; Sage.

Hackney Council (not dated) *RESPECT* (an educational pack for primary and secondary schools) London; Hackney Council.

Hague, G and Malos, E (1996) *Tackling Domestic Violence: a Guide to Developing Multi-agency Initiatives* Bristol; The Policy Press.

Hague, G, Kelly, L, Malos, E and Mullender, A with Debbonaire, T (1996) *Children, Domestic Violence and Refuges: a Study of Needs and Responses* Bristol; Women's Aid Federation of England.

Hester, M, Humphries, J, Pearson, C, Qaiser, K, Radford, L and Woodfield, K-S (1994) 'Domestic violence and child contact' in Mullender, A and Morley, R (eds) *Children Living with Domestic Violence: Putting Men's Abuse of Women on the Child Care Agenda* London;Whiting and Birch.

Hester, M and Pearson, C (1998) *From Periphery to Centre: Domestic Violence in Work with Abused Children* Bristol; The Policy Press.

Hester, M, Pearson, C and Harwin, N (1999) *Making an Impact: Children and Domestic Violence – a Reader* London; Jessica Kingsley.

Hester, M, Pearson, C and Harwin, N (1998) *Making an Impact: Children and Domestic Violence – a Training Pack* University of Bristol School for Policy Studies, NSPCC and Barnardos (with the involvement of the Women's Aid Federation of England) for the Department of Health (from: NSPCC National Training Centre, 3 Gilmour Close, Beaumont Leys, Leicester LE4 1EZ; price: £120.00).

Hester, M and Radford, L (1996) *Domestic Violence and Child Contact in England and Denmark* Bristol; Policy Press.

Home Office (1992) *Criminal Statistics: England and Wales* 1990 London; HMSO (and annually thereafter).

Home Office (1994) *National Guidelines for Family Court Welfare Work* London; Home Office.

*Housing Act* (1996) London; HMSO.

Hughes, H (1992) 'Impact of spouse abuse on children of battered women' *Violence Update* 1 August, pp.9–11.

Humphreys, C (2000) *Social Work, Domestic Violence and Child Protection: Challenging Practice*, Bristol: Policy Press.

Humphreys, C and Mullender, A.(forthcoming) Making Links: working with domestic violence? in Horwarth, J. and Shardlow, S. (eds.) *Making Links: Assessment and Roles across Specialisms,* Lyme Regis: Russell House Publishing.

Imam, U F (1994) 'Asian children and domestic violence' in Mullender, A and Morley, R (eds) *Children Living with Domestic Violence: Putting Men's Abuse of Women on the Child Care Agenda* London; Whiting and Birch.

James, A, Jenks, C and Prout, A (1998) *Theorizing Childhood* Cambridge; Polity Press.

Jaffe, P G, Wolfe, D A and Wilson, S K (1990) *Children of Battered Woman*, Newbury Park, CA: Sage.

Kelly, L (1994) 'The interconnectedness of domestic violence and child abuse: challenges for research, policy and practice' in Mullender, A and Morley, R (eds) *Children Living with Domestic Violence: Putting Men's Abuse of Women on the Child Care Agenda* London; Whiting and Birch.

Kelly, L (1999) *Domestic Violence Matters: An Evaluation of a Development Project* Home Office Research Study 193, London; Home Office.

Leeds City Council Department of Education and Leeds Inter-Agency Project (date not known) *Guidance for Schools: Violence against Women and Children by Known Men* Leeds; Leeds City Council Department of Education.

London Borough of Hackney (1993) *The Links between Domestic Violence and Child Abuse: Developing Services* London; London Borough of Hackney.

London Borough of Islington (1995a) *Working with Those Who Have Experienced Domestic Violence: a Good Practice Guide* (revised version) London; London Borough of Islington, Women's Equality Unit.

London Borough of Islington (1995b) *STOP: Schools Take On Preventing Domestic Violence* London; London Borough of Islington, Women's Equality Unit.

Loosley, S, Bentley, L, Lehmann, P, Marshall, L, Rabenstein, S and Sudermann, M (1997) *Group Treatment for Children Who Witness Woman Abuse: A Manual for Practitioners* London, Ontario; The Community Group Treatment Program. (available from: The Children's Aid Society of London and Middlesex, P.O. Box 6010, Depot 1, London, Ontario, Canada N5W 5R6).

Malos, E, Hague, G and Dear, W (1996) *Multi-agency Work and Domestic Violence: a National Study of Inter-agency Initiatives* Bristol; The Policy Press.

Mama, A (1996) *The Hidden Struggle: Statutory and Voluntary Sector Responses to Violence against Black Women in the Home* (reissue) London; Whiting and Birch.

Marshall, L, Miller, N, Miller-Hewitt, S, Sudermann, M, Watson, L, (1995) *Evaluation of Groups for Children who have Witnessed Violence* London; Ontario: Centre for Research on Violence Against Women and Children.

Mathews, D J (1995) 'Parenting groups for men who batter' in Peled, E, Jaffe, P G and Edleson, J L (1995) *Ending the Cycle of Violence: Community Responses to Children of Battered Women* Thousand Oaks, California; Sage.

Maynard, M (1985) 'The response of social workers to domestic violence' in Pahl, J *Private Violence and Public Policy: The Needs of Battered Women and the Response of the Public Services* London; Routledge and Kegan Paul.

McGee, C (forthcoming) *Children's Experiences of Domestic Violence* London: Jessica Kingsley.

Mezey, G C (1997) 'Domestic violence and pregnancy' *British Journal of Obstetrics and Gynaecology* 104, May, pp.528–531.

Milner, J (1993) 'A disappearing act: the differing career paths of fathers and mothers in child protection investigations' *Critical Social Policy* 13, pp.48–63.

Mooney, J (1994) *The Hidden Figure: Domestic Violence in North London* London; London Borough of Islington, Police and Crime Prevention Unit (or from Middlesex University, Centre for Criminology).

Morran, D and Wilson, M (1997) *Men Who are Violent to Women: a Groupwork Practice Manual* Lyme Regis; Russell House Publishing.

Morley, R and Mullender, A (1994) 'Domestic violence and children: what do we know from research?' in Mullender, A and Morley, R (eds) *Children Living with Domestic Violence: Putting Men's Abuse of Women on the Child Care Agenda* London; Whiting and Birch.

Mullender, A (1994a) 'Groups for child witnesses of woman abuse: learning from North America' in Mullender, A and Morley, R (eds) *Children Living with Domestic Violence: Putting Men's Abuse of Women on the Child Care Agenda* London; Whiting and Birch.

Mullender, A (1994b) 'School-based work: education for prevention' in Mullender, A and Morley, R (eds) *Children Living with Domestic Violence: Putting Men's Abuse of Women on the Child Care Agenda* London; Whiting and Birch.

Mullender, A (1996) *Rethinking Domestic Violence: the Social Work and Probation Response* London; Routledge.

Mullender, A, Debbonaire, T, Hague, G, Kelly, L and Malos, E (1998) 'Working with children in women's refuges' *Child and Family Social Work* 3, pp. 87–98.

Mullender, A and Humphreys, C with Saunders, H (1998) *Child Protection and Domestic Violence* London; Local Government Association.

Mullender, A, Hague, G, Imam, U, Kelly, L and Malos, E with Regan, L. (forthcoming) *'It Makes me Sad': Children's Perspectives on Domestic Violence* London; Sage.

Mullender, A and Morley, R (eds) (1994) *Children Living with Domestic Violence: Putting Men's Abuse of Women on the Child Care Agenda* London; Whiting and Birch.

NCH Action for Children (1994) *The Hidden Victims: Children and Domestic Violence* London; NCH Action for Children.

Northamptonshire County Council (not dated) *Relationships Without Fear* (Resource Pack for Schools) Northampton; Northamptonshire County Council, Education and Libraries.

O'Hara, M (1994) 'Child deaths in contexts of domestic violence: implications for professional practice' in Mullender, A and Morley, R (eds) *Children Living with Domestic Violence: Putting Men's Abuse of Women on the Child Care Agenda* London; Whiting and Birch.

Peled, E and Davis, D (1995) *Group Work with Children of Battered Women* Beverly Hills, CA; Sage.

Peled, E and Edleson, J L (1995) 'Process and outcome in groups for children of battered women' in Peled, E, Jaffe, P G and Edleson, J L (1995) *Ending the Cycle of Violence: Community Responses to Children of Battered Women* Thousand Oaks, California; Sage.

Pence, E and Paymar, M (1988) *Education Groups for Men who Batter: the Duluth Model* New York; Springer.

Pence, E and Paymar, M (1990) *Power and Control: Tactics of Men Who Batter. An Educational Curriculum* (revised edition) Duluth, Minnesota; Minnesota Program Development, Inc. (from 206 West Fourth Street, Duluth, MN 55806, USA).

*Protection from Harassment Act* (1997) London; HMSO

Radford, J (1992) 'Womanslaughter: a license to kill? The killing of Jane Asher' in Radford, J and Russell, D (eds) *Femicide: The Politics of Woman Killing* Buckingham; Open University.

Stanko, E A, Crisp, D, Hale, C and Lucraft, H (1998) *Counting the Costs: Estimating the Impact of Domestic Violence in the London Borough of Hackney* Swindon; Crime Concern (from: Crime Concern, Signal Point, Station Road, Swindon SN1 1FE).

Sudermann, M, Jaffe, P G and Hastings, E (1995) 'Violence prevention programs in secondary (high) schools' in Peled, E, Jaffe, P G and Edleson, J L (1995) *Ending the Cycle of Violence: Community Responses to Children of Battered Women* Thousand Oaks, California; Sage.

Widom, C S (1989) 'Does violence beget violence? A critical examination of the literature' *Psychological Bulletin* 106(1), pp. 3–28.

Williams, O. (1994) 'Healing and confronting the African American man who batters' in Carillo, R. and Tello, J. (eds.) *Healing the Male Spirit: Men of Color and Domestic Violence*, New York; Springer.

Wilson, M and Daly, M (1992) *Homicide*, New York; Aldine de Gruyter.

Wolfe, D A, Zak, L, Wilson, S and Jaffe, P (1986) 'Child witnesses to violence between parents: critical issues in behavioural and social adjustment' *Journal of Abnormal Child Psychology* 14(1), pp.95–104.

Women's Aid Federation of England (1998) *Annual Report* Bristol; WAFE.

Yearnshire, S (1996) 'Men of violence' *Police Review* 30 August, pp.28–29.

**Dilemmas of Financial Assessment**   *Greta Bradley & Jill Manthorpe*

The implementation of the NHS and Community Care Act 1990 has impacted on the lives of service user‌ s one important area of change: the increasi‌ HAVERING COLLEGE OF F & H E circumstances in order to maximise their in‌ ‌ ‌ ‌ ‌ ‌ o pay for services. For many social worker‌ ‌ ed social workers feel anxious and torn bet‌ ‌ ‌ ‌ ‌ ‌ 161220 ‌ ‌ ‌ community care and the values they associate with traditional social work tasks.

**ISBN: 1 873878 90 7**

**Down's Syndrome and Dementia**   *Diana Kerr*

This book defines good practice in needs assessment and the provision of services for the growing number of people with Down's Syndrome and Dementia. It is based on a social model which demands that we see the person first and the disease second. It gives many practical examples of ways in which workers and carers can intervene to support people and avoid behaviour and practices which disempower and can harm. It will be relevant to social workers, social care workers, community nurses, carers, staff in supported accommodation and anyone working in community settings.

**ISBN: 1 86178 017 6**

**Drugs, Children and Families**   *Jane Mounteney & Harry Shapiro*

This book aims to demystify the drug phenomenon, and increase social workers' knowledge of drug use, by providing a range of up-to-date information about drugs and their effects, by exploring ways drug use may arise as an issue for clients and social services departments and through exploration of a range of social work interventions. *Drugs, Children and Families* draws on relevant research where this exists and highlights a number of concerns, particularly in relation to interventions and provision for young people with drug use problems.

**ISBN: 1 86178 013 3**

**Family Support**   *Ruth Gardner*

Family support has attracted much less attention in terms of research and development than the more clearly defined systems for children in need of statutory protection and/or those looked after by local authorities. Yet it is a legal requirement of the Children Act (England and Wales) 1989, backed up by the UN Convention on the Rights of the Child. This book describes the essential elements of good family support and gives examples of research, planning, budget management and evaluated practice. It is essential reading for managers and practitioners, commissioning or providing these services, in all settings.

**ISBN: 1 86178 026 5**

**Poverty**   *Monica Dowling*

This ethnographic study of two social work teams combines a participant observation study of social workers with an analysis of the relationship between poverty and social work. It also incorporates findings from a three year qualitative study of social service users' and carers' experiences of community care. The book develops an unusual eclectic approach by applying psychological, sociological and social policy constructs to the study of of poverty and social; work. In conclusion it points the way forward for future social work practice, policy and research in relation to issues of financial deprivation and social exclusion.

**ISBN: 1 86178 025 7**